Additional Praises for
Expert Fraud Investigation: A Step-by-Step Guide

"Crime is inherently dramatic. And since fraud is a crime, writing about the subject of fraud should not be mundane nor monotonous but rather riveting, exciting and informative. Tracy Coenen, in her new book *Expert Fraud Investigation: A Step by Step Guide*, may be the first to actually capture why the topic of fraud is not only exciting but also informative, thought provoking and most importantly a subject that no one can afford to not thoroughly understand. In an environment of fraud on Wall Street and on Main Street, this book literally levels the playing field by equipping everyone who wants to avoid becoming a future fraud victim. In times like these, this is a must read."

—Barry Minkow, Co-Founder Fraud Discovery Institute

"This book should be required reading for anyone who is thinking about or is about to start on their fraud examiners career. She doesn't talk down to the reader but lays out in clear concise points that must be considered before starting ones own firm as well as a fraud investigation. This is where Tracy's experience and knowledge about fraud shine through.

She continuously establishes credibility with the season fraud examiner by being subtle yet informative with her own opinion which is based on years of practical experience. It is evident this book is not written by a college professor looking for tenure at a University. Instead it appears to be written by a seasoned professional with years of experience. I would strongly recommend it to the experienced fraud professional as well as it contains information needed throughout ones career."

—David Bleser, President, Bleser & Associates, LLC

"Ms. Coenen's book should be on every accounting and financial manager's bookshelf. When you suspect fraud, call an expert. But this book explains the who, what, where, and why of financial frauds and the techniques professionals like Ms. Coenen use to help you investigate and prosecute it."

—Francine McKenna, President,
McKenna Partners LLC and Author of the blog,
re: The Auditors

"Through an examination of common types of frauds and discussion of 'best practice' methods to identify fraud, this book provides excellent practical guidance on how to conduct a fraud examination. Such guidance is a valuable resource to auditors and security professionals involved in fraud examinations. I highly recommend this book to auditors, security professionals, management and board of directors who desire a practical, not theoretical, understanding of fraud examinations."

—Michael D. Akers, PhD, CFE, CPA, Professor and Chair,
Department of Accounting-Marquette University,
Charles T. Horngren Professor of Accounting

Expert Fraud Investigation

Expert Fraud Investigation

A Step-by-Step Guide

TRACY L. COENEN

WILEY

John Wiley & Sons, Inc.

Published by John Wiley & Sons, Inc., Hoboken, New Jersey.
Published simultaneously in Canada.

For general information on our other products and services, or technical support, please
contact our Customer Care Department within the United States at 800-762-2974, outside
the United States at 317-572-3993 or fax 317-572-4002.

Wiley also publishes its books in a variety of electronic formats. Some content that
appears in print may not be available in electronic books.

For more information about Wiley products, visit our web site at www.wiley.com.

Library of Congress Cataloging-in-Publication Data:

Coenen, Tracy, 1972–
    Expert fraud investigation : a step-by-step guide / Tracy L. Coenen.
        p. cm.
    Includes index.
    ISBN 978-0-470-38796-2 (cloth)
    1. Fraud.   2. Investigations.   I. Title.
    HV6691.C54 2009
    363.25'963–dc22

                                                            2008040311

10 9 8 7 6 5 4 3 2 1

For Grandma & Grandpa

Contents

Preface

Fraud investigation is a field that has gotten plenty of publicity since the big public company frauds uncovered in the early 2000s. Despite the media coverage and overall greater awareness of the issue, there are few books to date that have led readers through the process of conducting a fraud investigation. *Expert Fraud Investigation: A Step-by-Step Guide* changes all of that. It is the first book to really make the leap from theoretical discussion of fraud investigations to the actual nuts and bolts of performing an investigation.

This book is no substitute for real-world experience under the direction of a highly qualified forensic accountant or fraud investigator, but it is a tool to help professionals learn about fraud investigations. This guide takes the professional through the process of opening an investigation, selecting a team, gathering data, and the entire investigation.

It discusses the most common types of fraud cases, and points out some of the best methods for analyzing the books and records to search for proof of fraud. Business executives, auditors, and security professionals will benefit from this book, and companies should find this a useful tool for fighting fraud within their own organizations.

The basis for this book is more than a decade of fraud investigation experience, with cases ranging from those at small family-owned companies to large publicly traded corporations. Formal and informal training have helped refine my fraud investigation skills and add to my repertoire of techniques to ferret out fraud.

Acknowledgments

Thank you again to everyone at Wiley who has helped make writing this book easier than I ever imagined. You allow me the creative freedom to write according to my vision, and for that, I can't thank you enough. It is an honor to be associated with such professionals.

I again thank my family, friends, and business associates, who support and encourage me each day. Special thanks goes out to Max, who makes each day worth living. You are the best!

CHAPTER 1

Finding Fraud

There are two different ways that a reactive fraud investigation starts. One type of investigation begins when an actual fraud has been identified, and maybe one or more perpetrators are identified, too. The other type of investigation starts with a strong suspicion of fraud, but no real proof of theft.

Both types of investigations are important to any organization that takes fraud prevention and control seriously. Companies with good fraud prevention controls actively monitor their systems and follow up on questionable data and unusual relationships between numbers. The investigation that starts this way should not be viewed as any less important than the one that begins with a definitive instance of fraud.

Signs of Fraud

Numerous signs can point to the possibility of fraud. Literally hundreds of different types of fraud schemes exist, so the number of possible red flags of fraud is huge. It would be impossible to cover them all in their entirety here, but some general signs of fraud can apply across all types of businesses and fraud schemes.

It is important to educate management and employees on these warning signs of fraud. Study after study indicates that tips from employees are one of the most common ways that corporate fraud is detected. Therefore, it makes sense to educate employees about symptoms of fraud so they can report red flags when they see them.

Accounting Irregularities

Irregularities that point to the possibility of fraud can range from simple things like unreconciled accounts and unusual account balances to more complex problems like "on-top entries," which are made after the books are closed in order to manipulate the numbers ultimately reported on the financial statements.

An auto dealership had a controller who had not reconciled the bank accounts for nearly a year, despite management's insistence that it be done. Management did not insist enough, and the problem persisted; the accounts remained unreconciled month after month. Unreconciled bank accounts usually signal one of two problems: The accounting staff is incompetent or understaffed, or there is a fraud-in-progress that will likely be exposed through a bank reconciliation. Both of these problems need to be corrected quickly.

In this case, it turned out that the controller simply couldn't handle all of the responsibilities of her job. She was out of her league and was not doing the reconciliations because she did not have time and was likely afraid that the reconciliations would expose her incompetence. The reconciliations would have shown that she didn't have a good handle on the company's finances.

The auto dealership was lucky in this case. They simply dismissed the controller and hired someone more experienced and more competent. But there was a period of time during which management was afraid a fraud had occurred. They should have recognized early on that the unreconciled accounts were a sign of a big problem.

Cynthia Cooper, head of internal audit at WorldCom, recounts the on-top entries problem that she and her team discovered was part of a massive fraud scheme at the company. Executives were directing employees to make journal entries *on top* of the regular general ledger activity to make the financial statements conform to a predetermined template. Lower-level employees did not see these entries, because they occurred outside the regular system of recording accounting details, so the practice went on for a long time before it was discovered.

To further confuse anyone who might look at the on-top entries, executives directed a web of confusing entries to be made. They were not a handful of simple debits and credits. There were hundreds of entries, with figures divided and bounced between many different accounts, apparently in an attempt to confuse and discourage anyone who might try to dig into these entries. The existence of these entries was discovered because of some irregular numbers and account names by the internal audit team. This demonstrates the importance of being on the lookout for unusual accounts, numbers, and descriptions within the accounting system.

It's not always easy to spot accounting irregularities. After all, an employee or executive who engages in fraud is often aware of what others are expecting their work or their numbers to look like. In many companies, management knows that revenue and expenses are expected to fall within certain parameters. Numbers outside of those expectations might raise suspicions. So a good fraudster will ensure that the numbers do not appear unusual in that regard. It's only when someone digs deeper that the irregularities start to surface. An examination of a public company's Securities and Exchange Commission (SEC) filings might reveal some notes or disclosures that do not make sense in light of the numbers reported. Small clues like these will be necessary to point to irregularities.

For example, suppose a company reports in the notes to the year-end financial statements that the raw materials used to make its products have become significantly more expensive. An examination of the company's gross profit margin, however, shows that the percentage is stable. The only legitimate way for the gross profit percentage to remain unchanged during a period in which raw material prices increase significantly is for the sales price of the goods to rise proportionately. The sales prices at this company did not change, however, so that immediately raises a red flag about that unchanged gross profit margin. The numbers reported don't make sense in light of the information provided in the notes. This should definitely be examined further.

It is clear that the accounting irregularities giving rise to a fraud investigation may not be easily identifiable. Those committing financial statement fraud are often adept at covering their tracks, so the red flags are not always obvious. The investigator often relies on intuition when examining the numbers and explanations for possible irregularities.

Apparent Control Weaknesses

When readily apparent major deficiencies in a company's control procedures are identified, they should be considered warning signs that fraud could be occurring. All companies have some things that are not as secure as they should be. However, when the controls over a company's assets and data are severely deficient, that is cause for alarm.

Some of the most common characteristics that might be considered severe deficiencies include:

- *Complete lack of segregation of critical duties*, giving one or more persons almost complete control over a financial area of a company and offering many opportunities to commit fraud and easily conceal it. For example, if the same person receives customer payments, records the payments to the customer's accounts, makes the bank deposits, and reconciles the bank statement, there are many opportunities to commit and conceal fraud. The employee could steal a customer payment, record the payment on the customer's account so the customer doesn't know the funds have been stolen, and later adjust the accounting records while doing the bank reconciliation in order to cover the theft. If these duties are segregated among two or three employees, the risk of theft of a customer payment and subsequent acts to cover the theft are much less likely.
- *Ability to override controls and limits of authority easily*, either with no oversight of the process or with lax enforcement of it. For example, an area supervisor regularly exceeds his authority for vendor payments. His approval limit is capped at $20,000. He commonly requests that vendors issue multiple invoices for work, so that no individual invoice exceeds the $20,000 threshold. Upper management is aware of this situation, but does not enforce the policy or regularly monitor this

supervisor's activities. By failing to enforce the policy, management may be effectively encouraging the employee to continue to break rules, which could create opportunities for fraud.

- *Failure to reconcile accounts regularly.* Account reconciliation is important for accurate record keeping, even in the absence of fraud. Obviously, without reconciliations, management cannot know whether the books and records are accurate. Failure to reconcile also can encourage theft by employees who are aware that reconciliations are not done, and a theft could go unnoticed for a long time. In the example cited earlier in this chapter, management did not enforce its policy requiring monthly reconciliation of accounts, which led to a significant problem in the accounting function.

- *Poor accounting records in general.* This problem is often faced by smaller companies, but can also affect large companies, particularly ones that have done many acquisitions and have failed to integrate. Disjointed accounting systems make things difficult to monitor and reconcile, and offer opportunities for duplicate accounting entries to go unnoticed. Poor records also make it difficult for management to get an accurate financial picture of the company, and that could contribute to a fraud going unnoticed for a period of time.

It makes sense that the existence of major deficiencies in preventing fraud might be the precursor to fraud actually occurring at a company. If a company is lucky, it will catch the weaknesses before something happens. But many companies are not so lucky, and the identification of these types of problems should lead to further examination of the company to determine whether, in fact, fraud may have occurred under these serious circumstances.

If a company is not diligent about implementing good control procedures over its accounting function, it's also likely that management will not be interested in looking for the fraud that might result from the poor controls. Hopefully, internal or external fraud experts can encourage management to identify and examine the weaknesses and their results.

Another problem is that, when serious problems are found, a company often either ignores the problems or fixes them without looking into whether a defalcation is associated with the control weaknesses. As difficult as it may be for management to admit that weaknesses like this may have led to fraud, it is important to find out for sure what the fraud status is.

Lack of Information

When information and documentation is unavailable, it can raise questions about honesty or dishonesty. In the regular course of business, documents are sometimes lost or things cannot be explained. However, there comes a time when too many items are missing or the missing information is too suspicious to ignore.

For example, the bookkeeper of a nonprofit organization frequently had difficulty locating canceled checks that were requested by the auditors as part of their annual financial statement audits. The auditors instead relied on the information on the carbon copies in conjunction with the general ledger detail. Unfortunately, the payees noted on the carbon copies were not accurate, and the checks in question were actually issued to the bookkeeper. She destroyed these canceled checks as soon as the bank statement arrived, and hoped that the auditors wouldn't request copies of those specific checks.

When an occasional document is missing, it is usually not cause for alarm. But if a pattern of missing documentation emerges, it can be a warning sign of fraud. Look for missing information of a grouped or patterned nature: blocks of time, for a particular customer or vendor, for a certain type of transaction, or relating to a certain employee. A missing document or two is not all that disturbing, but ten missing documents, all related to one vendor—and all being questioned by management—are bothersome.

Apparent Deception

When people seem to be going out of their way to conceal information, alter documentation, or otherwise engage in behavior designed to deceive those looking for facts (auditors, superiors, investigators, etc.), it raises suspicions about fraud.

For example, a disability insurance claimant fills out all paperwork, but does not mention her ownership interest in a business that is closely related to the job that she is currently unable to perform. A fraud investigator discovers the business ownership independently and becomes suspicious that the claimant may actually be working in this business, even though she claims she cannot work at her regular job due to disability. This ownership interest merits additional scrutiny. People often don't hide things like this without good reason. It is possible that the claimant wanted to hide this ownership interest because it might lead to the investigator finding out she was working there. If she was not working there, and there was truly nothing to hide, why conceal it?

The same goes for deceptions in any type of fraud investigation or audit. It is presumed that if people are not honest about their involvement in situations, ownership of assets, professional licensing, or other material facts, they may have something to hide. Investigators should take clues like this very seriously. Lying is usually not compartmentalized. A deception in one area of life or a business is not usually an isolated incident. Take deception—either with outright lies or through the deliberate omission of critical information—as a likely sign of other problems.

Tips about Fraud

Companies rely heavily on reports about questionable behavior from employees, customers, vendors, or other outside parties. Tips are one of the most common ways that fraud is detected by companies, so any credible tip should be taken very seriously.

How does a company evaluate the credibility of a tip? It does not generally matter whether the tipster is anonymous, although it's reasonable to believe that those willing to put their names behind information do bring some measure of credibility to the information they are providing. Reliable tips usually have a sufficient amount of detail as to be believable. The more vague the tip is, the less reliable it is likely to be. The information provided by the tipster should also make sense in light of known circumstances surrounding the company's operation and the accused.

For example, a tip that merely states that Joe in the shipping department is acting like something unusual is going on is probably not very credible. In contrast, a report that Joe in shipping was seen in the shipping area several hours after his shift was over is a more specific tip that may be more reliable. If Joe was reported to be in the shipping and receiving area at a time when he is normally not working, and the door of the loading dock is open, this level of detail adds credibility to the report.

People do sometimes report false information in order to cause trouble for an enemy, an ex-spouse, or a disliked coworker, however. It is important to assess the potential motivation of a tipster when evaluating the information.

Change in Behavior or Lifestyle

When an employee exhibits significant changes in behavior, this is a potential sign of fraud. Drug and alcohol problems could be precursors to fraud because of the expense of addiction, or they could be the result of fraud as a person tries to hide a guilty conscience.

Behavioral changes, such as becoming uncooperative, argumentative, or defensive, can be signs of problems as well. These behaviors may be signs of dissatisfaction at work, which could be a reason for an employee to commit fraud. Or they could be an outward sign of an employee's stress as she or he engages in on-the-job fraud.

Newfound wealth is often difficult for a person to hide. Despite an employee's best efforts to keep a fraud under wraps, buying a new car or fancy jewelry may be too much to resist. Spending beyond one's apparent means should be a warning sign that a fraud may be occurring.

Management at a small company was surprised when the bookkeeper arrived at work one day on a brand-new Harley-Davidson motorcycle. Employees knew this was an expensive bike, and there was a general feeling that the bookkeeper and her husband weren't in a position to afford this luxury item. No one voiced their concerns to anyone else, because they did not want to seem judgmental about the bookkeeper's financial choices. They thought they ought to mind their own business.

Less than a year later, management discovered that the bookkeeper had been engaged in a long-term scheme to defraud the company. This fraud scheme was apparently the source of funds used to buy the Harley-Davidson. Had management investigated this unusual situation immediately, the company might have saved tens of thousands of dollars lost to theft after that luxury purchase.

None of these lifestyle changes alone is a definite indicator that fraud is occurring. Even several of these characteristics identified in one employee may not mean that a fraud is in progress. However, these signs are small pieces of a puzzle, and they should be watched carefully, because they are sometimes related to an occupational fraud.

Investigative Intuition

The least scientific of all the signs that fraud could be occurring may be the gut feeling that something is not right. Seasoned fraud investigators often refer to a "sixth sense" they get when examining situations and documents. This intuition is important in identifying instances of fraud and in looking for avenues to investigate in a suspected fraud scheme. Look for facts and relationships that don't make sense. Analyze relationships between people and between facts that seem unusual or counterintuitive. Find behavior that seems suspicious or out-of-the-ordinary.

A hunch, suspicion, feeling, or intuition requires further information and examination of data. When an investigator has developed her or his intuition related to fraud investigations, she or he cannot ignore the signs and fail to gather further information. Investigative intuition is a skill that can be developed over time and can be invaluable in fraud investigations.

Looking for Suspects

Those aware of fraud risks might think they should be on the lookout for likely fraud suspects. That is not a bad idea, and there are many potential personal red flags of fraud, but it is difficult to put those who commit fraud into one little box. Many different types of people commit fraud; it is difficult to pinpoint a few types who are more likely to steal from their employers.

It's important to recognize that there are inherently bad people who look for situations in which to take advantage of others. Companies try to avoid hiring these people but do not always weed them out because they may be good actors who are able to cover their evil intent. More likely, a company is a victim of a situational fraudster—someone who has a particular reason to commit a fraud at a certain time. This person would not normally be considered a bad or unethical person, but circumstances at home or work may motivate the employee to commit fraud.

A wide range of factors could cause a person to turn to fraud, including a legitimate financial need, a plan to get revenge on someone, a house going into foreclosure, a child support or alimony burden, an expensive addiction to drugs, a desire to engage in risky behavior for a thrill, or a feeling of power desired by the employee.

The motivators don't necessarily have to be evil-sounding. They can be everyday stresses and burdens that people find themselves suscep-tible to. Whatever the reasons or personal characteristics of a person who commits fraud, management will often be surprised by the identity of the dishonest employee. It is most often someone who was trusted and widely regarded as a good employee. It is only logical that the trusted employees would have access and opportunity to commit fraud. Managers typically do not provide access to information and assets for employees they don't trust. Only the trusted employees can access the bank accounts and look at confidential information—exactly the type of access that is needed to commit fraud.

When a doctor finds that her longtime bookkeeper has been stealing from her medical practice, she is often shocked. This was the woman she trusted for years to make the bank deposits, send out the bills, and generally handle the finances. How and why did fraud happen? Most often, that trust created between a business owner and an employee is exploited for financial gain. The bookkeeper knows the doctor is not looking at the bank statements, and therefore will not identify improper payments. The doctor does not have a good feel for the volume that is billed each month, and will not notice if the bookkeeper steals some cash payments from patients. The doctor trusted the bookkeeper to handle the money, and the employee was probably loyal and worthy of trust for years. But the combination of little oversight by the doctor and a personal financial need could cause an honest bookkeeper to turn to fraud.

A situation like this illustrates just how easy it is for an owner or executive to be defrauded by the least likely suspect. It is important to be aware of red flags that fraud may be occurring, and it is even more important to implement controls and oversights to prevent even the most seemingly honest employees from committing fraud.

Evaluating Fraud Tips

One of the most common ways that an internal fraud is detected is through a tip, from either an employee, a customer, a vendor, or an outside party. Anonymous hotlines are excellent tools for reporting fraud, but management must have a plan for evaluating these tips.

Some tipsters are okay with revealing their identities from the start. Others fear retribution or damage to their own reputations, so they prefer anonymous reporting. Just because a tip is anonymous, that does not mean it is any less credible than an allegation made by someone who is open about her or his identity. However, if someone is willing to reveal her or his identity when providing a tip, it may lend additional credibility to the information. Employees are sometimes worried that a hotline or other anonymous reporting mechanism might lead people to make false reports about others. While this does happen sometimes, those reports usually appear suspicious and are quickly identified as meritless.

Legitimate tips usually have specific (rather than general) allegations, sufficient information as to be believable, and a fact pattern that seems to fit with known variables in the workplace (the facts make sense). For example, a tip that indicates Janet in accounting is stealing customer payments would seem unreliable if Janet's job duties are such that she never comes into contact with customer payments. Management may want to verify that Janet does not have unintended access to those funds. If it can be verified that she does not have any access (authorized or unauthorized), the tip can likely be ruled out as bogus.

In contrast, if a report comes in that William in accounting is issuing payments to a fake company, and he is the employee who regularly generates accounts payable checks, that tip seems to make sense. The details will have to be investigated, but it is immediately clear that this fraud is possible given William's job duties.

How does management handle a tip? It is not wise to immediately dismiss the allegations, even if they seem completely baseless or are likely a hoax. In those cases, management should do some preliminary verification of facts. If this initial work completely debunks what was reported, it is probably okay to not investigate further. If the fact-checking finds that some or all of the representations in the tip are true, however, then further investigation is definitely warranted. The more facts that check out and the more serious the allegations, the more management should consider a formal investigation.

Suppose that a tip comes in about Amy, a commissioned salesperson, creating bogus sales at the end of the month to increase her monthly commissions. Management has noticed that commission payouts have been a bit higher than normal, and that the number of canceled orders has been unusually high. If Amy was causing false orders to be entered into the system, that would cause the commission payouts to be higher than they should. Higher-than-normal order cancellations could be related to Amy canceling orders after the month is closed and the commissions are calculated.

Management could then take the additional step of querying the accounting system to see whose customer orders are being canceled. If Amy's cancellations seem unusually high compared to everyone else's, this is another indicator that the tip may be credible. There is enough information backing up the allegations from the tipster, such that management should continue to look into the potential that a fraud is occurring.

Should You Investigate?

When an internal fraud occurs at a company, the natural reaction is to assume that an investigation must be started immediately. After all, it is important to determine who was involved, exactly how the fraud was committed and covered, and what evidence exists to prove the fraud.

Intuitively, that makes sense. In reality, it's not always the way things go. Whether a fraud is fully investigated often depends on the estimated size of the fraud and the size of the company in question. It does not always make sense for a company to investigate a fraud because of the cost involved.

For a public company, an internal fraud is probably always going to be investigated to some degree, and the larger the fraud, the larger the investigation. Many regulations must be followed, and it's imperative that financial statements be restated if necessary. To determine the amount of the fraud, the effect on the financial statements, and whether the financial statements need to be restated, an in-depth investigation is usually required.

But for private companies, it is not so certain that an investigation must be done. There are a variety of reasons why. It is important to first understand that the recovery of the proceeds of fraud is typically very small. The Association of Certified Fraud Examiners (ACFE) reports that in more than 65% of cases, 25% or less of the amount stolen is recovered.[1] So to undertake an investigation with the intention of recovering significant money from the thief is probably misguided. If a victim company is fortunate enough to have insurance coverage for the fraud, an investigation must be initiated to help compile a proper insurance claim with supporting documentation.

Yet there are times when an investigation should be done, even if money is unlikely to be recovered. Management may conduct an investigation because they are not sure who was involved in the fraud and need to identify all responsible parties. They may also be unsure of the exact methods used in the commission of the fraud, and an investigation will help nail down this aspect. Fraud investigations play an important part in fraud prevention efforts; finding out exactly how a fraud was perpetrated and who was involved can go a long way toward preventing future frauds.

Confronting Suspects

When management suspects a fraud has occurred, it is often difficult to decide whether to confront the suspect. Those who decide in favor of confrontation immediately start questioning the suspect. They usually have good intentions, but the situation can go wrong very quickly. Usually the goal is to gather information about the suspected fraud, and it is believed that confronting the suspect will accomplish this goal. That is the thinking of someone who is not experienced in fraud investigation.

Often there is only *one* chance to speak with a suspect about the situation, so it must be done carefully. Once management reveals its suspicions, the suspect often will not agree to future meetings, so no more information will be gathered from her or him. There is an art to interviewing suspects, as will be discussed in Chapter 6. It is best to leave these tenuous situations to the experts, or at the very least to someone who has some training in the field of interviewing.

Interviews with suspects are usually best done after the bulk of available information and evidence has been gathered and examined. Although human nature may cause us to want to start asking questions immediately, the better practice in most cases is to wait.

Skills of a Fraud Investigator

The educational background of a good fraud investigator can fall into a wide range of disciplines. Fraud investigators have degrees in accounting, finance, police science, law, or criminal justice. There is no widely accepted course of study for fraud investigators, although those degree programs that offer a strong foundation in accounting and finance seem to prepare students well for the numerical component of fraud investigations.

Many excellent fraud examiners have a work history that is far more important than their educational background. On-the-job experience as a police detective, federal agent, insurance claims analyst, financial statement auditor, or financial analyst can lend itself well to a career in fraud investigations. It's not unusual for practical experience in the field to play a much bigger part in the fraud investigator's skills than any type of classroom training. The field of fraud examinations has an extremely varied range of educational and work experience. Other careers often have a few well-defined career paths, but the road to success as a fraud investigator can lead in many directions.

A strong financial background includes a working knowledge of financial statements and possibly a good grasp of the accounting process. Many successful investigators come from a background that did not necessarily focus on the process of accounting, so it is obviously still possible to be a great investigator without these skills, but any accounting knowledge will enhance a fraud investigation.

A highly regarded forensic accountant or fraud investigator is able to go beyond the investigation and excels in presenting the findings both in writing and orally. The investigator obviously has to be able to communicate the findings in a way that laypeople will be able to understand. Most cases have a possibility of going to court, so the ability to testify well is important.

How does a fraud investigator know whether she or he will do well testifying in a deposition or trial? It is difficult to say until she or he has actually done it. However, if a person is afraid of speaking in public, it is probably not a good fit. Think of testifying as speaking in public with members of the audience heckling you. It is the opposing attorney's job to poke holes in your work and opinions, and it can often get contentious. If you fluster easily or have a hard time making yourself understood, you will likely have a hard time testifying.

In anticipation of testifying as an expert witness, a fraud investigator must be willing to build a strong curriculum vitae (CV). The CV is often the first thing by which an expert will be judged, so making a good impression here is helpful. That good impression is made by offering up proof of your expertise, including degrees, certifications, employment history, continuing professional education, memberships in professional organizations, and articles and books written. Each piece of information on the CV should be aimed at proving that you are a well-qualified expert in your field.

Good fraud investigators are able to combine technical expertise with creativity and a knack for finding key pieces of evidence. The creativity component becomes crucial when you are trying to devise ways of verifying information or finding new evidence. The fraud investigator has to have multiple ways to find information, and the information is not always found where ordinary people would expect it. A good fraud investigator can locate a publicly available database or government agency that might be able to verify a fact. She or he might find a new witness to a situation by carefully examining some unusual documents.

Authoritative accounting and auditing literature often refers to the "professional skepticism" required of financial statement auditors. It's important that auditors be critical when examining the numbers and evaluating information provided by management. The auditor should constantly be asking whether the information makes intuitive sense, whether the explanations are reasonable, whether other explanations are possible, and whether the information presented is in fact true.

A fraud investigator takes this professional skepticism to a higher level. Some investigators are even accused of being too suspicious or of being negative in general. More likely, fraud investigators are so used to looking for what is wrong or inappropriate, that they are more prone to be skeptical of explanations, alleged evidence, and the facts as they have been presented.

Differences between Audits and Investigations

Many forensic accountants and fraud investigators come from a traditional auditing background. It makes sense for an auditor to use her or his accounting and financial expertise in this way, because that foundation is absolutely critical for a high-quality financial investigation. It can be a natural fit for the person who is comfortable with numbers to move into a financial investigator position.

As already discussed, additional skills go into a fraud examination, including investigative techniques, interviewing techniques, financial data reconstruction, and much more. But a position as an outside auditor can be one of the best foundations for success in forensic accounting, because it offers the professional an opportunity to see financial statements and accounting departments in action.

Audits have never been designed to find fraud, and they likely will never be. They are designed to find errors and improper applications of accounting rules. Fraud, by its nature, is difficult to find during an audit, because steps have been taken by the actors in the fraud to conceal it. Fraudsters try to conceal a fraud from not only the company's management and owners but also the auditors. Familiarity with the company's operations and the auditing procedures will help an employee successfully conceal the fraud.

There are a handful of obvious differences between an audit and a fraud investigation. The process of performing an audit versus an investigation is quite different. Audits are often very standard, with the examination of certain financial statement items done on a routine basis. Certain procedures, such as inventory test counts and accounts receivable confirmation, are standard and do not vary a lot from engagement to engagement. The auditors are essentially looking for documentation that supports the accounting entries, but are not usually trying to verify the authenticity of the documentation or determine whether the transactions under examination are suspicious.

In contrast, fraud examinations are anything but routine, and this materially affects the planning and execution of the engagement. The most obvious difference between an audit and a fraud investigation is the lack of standard work programs for fraud investigations.

Audits are done largely based on standard work programs that outline areas of testing and examination. There are some differences in these work programs from audit to audit, based on client circumstances. Work is done on a test basis, with auditors selecting a sample of transactions within their predetermined scope. If those transactions pass the auditors' tests, it is essentially assumed that other transactions would pass the tests as well.

There is no such standardized process during a fraud examination. Checklists and investigation guides can help to some extent, but the investigative procedures are often determined based on the results of work just completed. Work is usually not done on a test basis. An area of suspicion is isolated, and the fraud investigator will usually examine all transactions within that area.

Audits rely heavily on the concept of materiality. Auditors regularly consider whether an item or transaction would make a difference in the eyes of the user of financial statements. Materiality is often defined largely in terms of dollars, but also involves circumstantial considerations that a financial statement user might consider important.

The SEC defines *materiality* as:

The omission or misstatement of an item in a financial report is material if, in the light of surrounding circumstances, the magnitude of the item is such that it is probable that the judgment of a reasonable person relying upon the report would have been changed or influenced by the inclusion or correction of the item.[2]

For example, in a company with annual sales of $10 billion, an improperly recorded sale of $25,000 likely would not make a difference to someone looking at the financial statements. It is just too small of a dollar amount to even matter when compared to total sales of $10 billion. In contrast, a theft of $25,000 at the same company committed by the CFO might be considered material, even though the dollar amount is equally as small as the first situation. In this case, the relative amount is small, but the theft could very well be considered material because it was perpetrated by the top finance official in the company. That executive is essentially in charge of the money at the company, and if he is stealing, that circumstance may be material.

Materiality is not relied on in fraud investigations to dismiss irregularities. Any size fraud may be important to the organization regardless of the dollar figure. Small thefts can easily be significant, because they might indicate larger problems within the company. They may also tip investigators off to other larger frauds. It is not as simple to dismiss small items in a fraud investigation as it is in a financial statement audit.

The other major difference between audits and investigations relates to the opinions expressed. Audits are aimed at giving negative assurance: The auditors are not aware of anything that would make the financial statements incorrect. Fraud examinations give positive assurance: We found X, Y, and Z during our examination, and here is the evidence.

Fraud investigations are regularly referred to as *fraud audits*, although that term really should be avoided because of the confusion it can cause. An *audit* is a specific type of service offered by accountants, and a fraud investigation is quite different from an audit. It is more appropriate to refer to the project as a *fraud investigation, fraud examination,* or *forensic accounting project.* While the terms used to describe this type of engagement seem like an insignificant matter, the most precise language possible should be used to describe your work.

Conducting a Fraud Investigation

The focus of this book is the actual performance of a fraud investigation. The challenge in educating the reader about investigations is the wide variety of cases that can be handled by fraud investigators. This book attempts to instruct readers on some of the most common fraud schemes, controls that can help prevent them, and techniques for detecting them.

We will talk at length about the many signs of financial fraud and techniques that fraud investigators can use to further examine a company's finances to determine whether a fraud has occurred. Remember that because there are so many different types of fraud schemes and continuously evolving technology, which creates new opportunities for fraud, no book could ever cover all possible situations. This book covers some of the most common schemes and investigative techniques.

The information in this book is for general and educational purposes only, and should not be construed as legal or accounting advice or opinion. The material in this book may or may not be applicable or suitable for your specific circumstances or needs. Fraud investigations should be conducted by professionals with sufficient competence and experience in the field. The information in this book should not be considered a substitute for work experience or supervision by management. Please consult with a qualified fraud investigation professional before taking any action based on the information in this book.

Notes

1. 2006 Report to the Nation on Occupational Fraud and Abuse, Association of Certified Fraud Examiners, Austin, TX.
2. SEC Staff Accounting Bulletin: No. 99—Materiality; www.sec.gov/interps/account/sab99.htm.

CHAPTER 2

Beginning the Investigation

After someone in charge decides that a fraud investigation is necessary, the process of creating a team, mapping the investigation plan, and requesting information begins. Obviously, a successful investigation is impossible without completing this part of the process competently. An organized approach is the best way to ensure that all facets of the investigation flow smoothly, that staff is properly assigned and supervised, and that all critical evidence is analyzed.

Many of the administrative parts of a forensic accounting or fraud investigation project are similar to those in a traditional auditing assignment. For those who have played an active role in managing audit engagements, some of this information will be familiar. Yet when it comes to the actual performance of the engagement, distinct differences must be highlighted. Probably the biggest difference between a fraud investigation and a traditional audit is that each investigation is so strikingly different from the last. There is not a standard roadmap for a fraud investigation, and each engagement will have many unique characteristics.

Traditional financial statement audits, however, are relatively similar from year to year unless a company has had a significant change in operations. Typically, the auditors rely heavily on the audit plan and audit workpapers from the prior year to guide their current-year work. That is a distinct advantage in the field, because the staff has these items to direct their work and help ensure that the audit is thorough.

Experience with traditional auditing and accounting engagements is a big plus when preparing for a fraud investigation. The key is not to rely too heavily on what you've done in the past. Rather, use that experience managing engagements as a foundation to create new ways of mapping out the work and supervising the staff. Try to develop a new investigative technique or become proficient with a method of analysis with each fraud investigation to enhance your skills as an investigator.

Assessing the Engagement

Even though different types of investigations will require different detailed steps and procedures, the mechanics of budgeting, planning, and assembling a team will be the same. A large investigation requires a greater deal of organization, but a smaller investigation still requires good process management and staff supervision, too. It would be a mistake to take planning lightly just because a case is small. It is still important to be sure that all critical items are investigated, and that investigation results are documented, no matter the size of the case.

Probably the most critical part of planning the engagement is determining exactly what needs to be investigated and what information and resources are available to the team. Without a clear definition of the problem and the expected outcomes, a fraud examination team cannot possibly meet a client's objectives. You have to know what those objectives are first.

Don't make the mistake of thinking that the client wants to accomplish what you want to accomplish. Most clients will not have experienced an internal fraud before, and they won't know where to start with an investigation. They will not know how little or how much investigating you can do, what the cost might be, what results they can expect, and what their legal rights are. It's up to the fraud examiner to present the options and educate the client about them.

Understanding the tasks to be completed involves a lot of listening, as the client will want to tell you what has led up to the need for an investigation, what information has been gathered to date, and what is at your disposal for your investigation. A fraud investigator might feel like she or he is also playing the part of counselor during an initial meeting. Especially in cases in which the suspected thief was a highly valued and trusted employee, management and owners of the company may be very upset. They are likely looking for reassurance from the investigator, a validation that fraud happens in many companies, and confidence that the investigation will help the company move forward.

In order to properly plan the investigation, the fraud investigator needs to be able to ask good questions that extract valuable information about what needs to be done. The specific questions vary with each investigation, but the following are some basic areas that an investigator will definitely want to touch on.

What happened?
- How did this situation come to light?
- Who was involved with the discovery?
- Who is aware that a potential fraud occurred?

Evidence
- What evidence has already been found?
- How conclusive is it?
- Are there multiple pieces of evidence?
- Might there be other easily discoverable pieces of evidence?
- How much does the evidence tell us about the methods of fraud and the parties involved?

Who is suspected?
- Who is the primary suspect?
- At what level is this person employed?
- Is she or he still employed with the company?
- Has the employee been suspended or terminated?
- Will the results of our investigation impact the employee's future with the organization?
- Who else do you think might be involved?
- Who else could be involved simply based on their access and opportunity to commit fraud?

- Do you think any employees were intimidated into participating in or facilitating the fraud?
- Is anyone suspected of helping to cover up the fraud?

Are outside parties involved?
- Does this fraud involve a vendor, a customer, or other outside party with which the company does business?
- What do we know about their involvement?
- Is their involvement limited to a single person, or does it extend to multiple parties or the company as a whole?
- Will they cooperate with our investigation?
- Do they have documentation that we might need?

Key players
- Who can explain the processes in the affected department or division?
- How are roles assigned in the department or division?
- Who is supervising?
- Who has critical information for us?
- Who can help gather information and documentation?
- Whom will we report to?
- Who else needs to be apprised of our progress?

Who knows?
- Who is aware that a potential fraud has taken place?
- Who needs to be informed (e.g., upper management, insurance carrier, board of directors, investors, bank, other interested parties)?

Secrecy
- Should we keep the fact that an investigation is being started quiet?
- Should only certain people know?
- Should work be performed off-site to minimize our impact on the organization?
- Is it necessary to be on-site for access to computers, documents, or key people?

- Will we be widely known as *fraud investigators*, or will we use a less threatening title such as *auditors*?

Data and documentation
- When can we begin to receive documentation?
- What is available to us?
- What format is it in (digital versus hardcopy)?
- What organizations have information that we may need (e.g., banks, investment firms, vendors)?
- How will we go about getting the information?
- Can an employee help gather documentation?
- Will we need to get signed authorizations to get information from outside parties?
- Do your employees need help identifying what we will need for the investigation?

What has already happened?
- Has management already tried to start its own investigation?
- What have they examined?
- Is the integrity of any evidence compromised?

Investigation goals
- What is our scope of work?
- What questions do you want answered?
- What level of certainty and precision do you want?
- Who will receive our report?
- What will our report be used for (e.g., civil litigation, criminal prosecution, insurance recovery)?
- Are you interested in remediation after the investigation ends?
- Would you like our recommendations for techniques and controls to prevent fraud in the future?

Clients may not necessarily be overflowing with information on these questions. Remember that they have probably never encountered fraud before, and this is new territory for them. Also, they may not volunteer this information and may need to be asked the specific questions.

It is important for the fraud investigator to guide this portion of the initial meeting and keep the conversation on topic. It is easy for the client to get distracted or to start drowning in the minutia of the situation. Details can be discussed later. This information-gathering session should be as broad as possible and allow the fraud investigator to gather answers to these introductory questions relatively easily.

When necessary, tell the client that you're going to make a note of some specifics that you will discuss with them later. This is a good way of acknowledging the client's concerns and affirming that you want their information, but it helps you keep the conversation moving in order that you may get through all of these questions.

Making Recommendations

Because of their lack of experience with fraud investigations, the client will rely on the fraud investigator's expertise to help guide the engagement. They are relying on the expert to tell them how the investigation happens and how the scope of work should be determined. Clients appreciate being informed, so it is a good idea to walk them through what will happen and then make regular updates during your work.

The lead investigator should not be afraid to make recommendations to the client. They often appreciate the guidance in terms of the scope and objectives of the investigation. One way to offer guidance is to propose three or four courses of action, with the depth of the investigation ranging from less extensive to more extensive. Help the client understand the expected outcome of each of those choices and the usefulness of the information developed throughout such investigations. Then make a recommendation based on the information you have gathered from exploring the aforementioned items. A client is almost always receptive to the recommendation and the reasons why that alternative is preferable.

For example, a case involving expense report fraud by the president of a company is often a time-intensive activity with little financial benefit. There are often hundreds or thousands of receipts and statements to sift through, and investigating several years of expense reports is often a costly process. There is a great chance that money stolen via expense reports will not be recovered, but the investigation is still important, because the proof of fraud is necessary to take action against the employee. If this is the case, it probably makes the most sense to examine only one year of expense reports. That should be enough to find proof of fraud (or not).

Examining three or five years' worth of expense reports is far more expensive, with little additional benefit. Either fraud occurred or it did not, and an examination of a shorter period can provide proof of that. Additional time periods can always be investigated if it is later deemed important. Walk the client through the logic behind this kind of situation. Most clients will appreciate the guidance and your willingness to help keep investigation costs down.

A fraud investigator's job is not to do as much work as possible, generate the highest possible fees, and keep the project going as long as possible. The investigator's job is to help the client get the most useful results from an investigation and make the most sensible investment of time and money. An experienced fraud investigator can almost always make a good recommendation in light of this scenario, offering advice on the most cost-effective and worthwhile course of action.

Sometimes a cost-benefit analysis shows that a complete, detailed investigation is not worth the price tag. Particularly when a client has little hope of recovering money, it may not make sense to conduct an extensive investigation. In this case, a limited-scope engagement with a few broad objectives may be better, such as correcting the financial statements, quantifying some obvious instances of theft, and doing a high-level examination of a few at-risk areas in the finance function.

There are other times when it does make sense to investigate in a very detailed fashion. A public company might be more likely to want a larger scope of work, or a company with a private shareholder group may want the accountability brought by a more detailed investigation.

More times than not, a middle-of-the-road approach works well. If too little work is done, too many vulnerabilities could go unnoticed. If too much work is done, there could be great expense without much return. A more moderate work plan ensures that the most egregious acts of fraud or the most risky areas of the company are examined. It allows management and owners to get a good understanding of what happened and who was involved, while controlling costs. More work can always be done if the situation warrants it, and it is advisable to include potential areas to be investigated in the future when creating your work plan for the investigation.

Budgeting and Cost Control

Planning the work to be performed during a fraud investigation requires that the project manager get an accurate assessment of the goal of the work and the documentation and resources available. It's important that the lead investigator not try to plan the work and the budget before gathering adequate information, because inevitably the budget will be inadequate and the work plan incomplete.

This is one area in which less experienced investigators make many mistakes. They are eager to secure a project and begin work, but are prone to overlook critical information in their haste. A good rule of thumb is to err on the side of asking too many questions and gathering too much preliminary information. That error is far less painful than making major decisions about the investigation based on too little information.

The initial meeting with a client is almost never the time to quote a fee, or even a range of fees for the project. The engagement manager runs the risk of quoting too high, which may cause the investigation team to lose the engagement before making a thorough assessment and proposal. If the quote is too low, the team will be in a difficult position later when a higher level of fees is quoted in the proposal. Clients are often quick to ask for a range of fees without giving the expert ample time and information to make a realistic determination. It is not out of line for the client to ask, because budgeting for a fraud investigation is almost always a big issue.

Resist the urge to answer this question prematurely. One way to handle a client who is interested in fees from the beginning is to tell the client that it would be unfair both to him and to the investigation team to make an estimate without the opportunity to really think through the work that needs to be performed. Explain that you need time to develop an approach to the investigation and to analyze the documents available to the investigators, and that you cannot possibly suggest an accurate fee range until after you've done that.

If that does not satisfy the client, it is possible to quote a wide range of fees based on other engagements of the same type that you have handled. There is the risk, however, that the client is paying attention only to the lower end of the range. The investigator is setting herself up for a challenge later if the actual fee comes in at the higher end of the range. Quoting a range early on is not the best approach, and should be done only if the client simply will not take no for an answer in the initial meeting.

It is important to find out whether the client has a budget (either preliminary or final) for the investigation. It is not the fraud investigator's job to spend the entire budget, so that is not why it is important to ask. It is important to inquire about the budget because it might be readily apparent that the client has unrealistic expectations or cannot afford the type of investigation the situation needs. By asking about the budget, the fraud investigator can address these expectations immediately and explain why a higher budget is necessary in order for a proper investigation to be done.

As with any engagement, the process of budgeting will require an assignment of staff and an estimate of the time required to complete the investigation. Of course, this is much easier on smaller engagements for which the work can be more easily defined. An experienced lead investigator will usually have no trouble estimating time requirements and assigning staff accordingly, and allowing some extra time for unexpected issues that may arise during the investigation.

Creating an accurate budget and controlling the costs accordingly will require close supervision of staff. Often, less experienced investigators are not adept at determining how much time to allocate to various tasks. They are not as comfortable deciding which things need close inspection versus those that need only a high-level examination. It is important to guide them in this regard so that work can stay within the budget.

The budget will probably be based largely on the volume of documentation to examine and the level of detail required. There is not a standard or a rule of thumb for estimating this, which is why experience in fraud investigations is so important when trying to budget. You will find that more experienced investigators are good at quickly getting a feel for the time commitment involved, but only because they have done so many investigations.

When creating a budget, do not overlook the potential that staff may have to reexamine documentation. It's not uncommon for a staff member to do a detailed examination of a set of documents, which is then reviewed by a supervisor. The supervisor finds that additional information needs to be extracted from the set of documents. A second detailed examination of the documents is needed, and there should be room in the budget for these things.

Experienced fraud investigators often have their own methods for budgeting and estimating time commitments. One critical part of budgeting for forensic accounting or fraud investigation projects is contingency planning. Experienced investigators may add 10% to 30% to their estimates based on their experience with time and cost overruns for the engagements they normally perform. Establishing this type of standard for your own firm or practice may take some time and experience, so it is not always as easy as it sounds.

Fees

Fraud investigators most often opt to bill their work on an hourly basis. Hourly fees are the norm for lawyers and accountants, so fraud examiners find that it is easiest to use this standard practice. There is not a whole lot to discuss in terms of hourly fees, because their use is so widespread, and it's a rather simple method of getting paid for your investigation. It is important to give careful consideration to your hourly fees.

Hourly fees have a huge range depending on the firm performing the work, the type of engagement, the experience level of the staff, and the geographic location of the client. It is not uncommon to see fees range from $100 per hour to several hundred dollars per hour. Some practitioners eagerly inquire with colleagues about their rates in order to assess their own billing norms. Gather information on rates of competitors if you can, and decide where you want to be positioned. Smaller firms are often interested in being low-cost leaders. They assume that clients are looking for the best bargain they can find, and because overhead is generally lower at small firms than at big firms, it might seem logical to pass the savings along to the client.

Even though this may be common, I do not recommend it be implemented in your practice. Do you really want to be seen as a low-cost leader? Do you want to be the "budget" forensic accountant that clients are looking for? Or would you rather offer fair fees that compensate you and your staff for the skills and expertise that you bring to the table?

Fees that offer a good value are better for the firm in many ways. Remember that part of the buying decision is a client's assessment of quality. Like it or not, the price paid goes a long way toward convincing customers that they are getting a high-quality product or service. Most clients are not looking for bargain-basement fraud investigators. They are looking for the best ones who charge fair fees.

One other consideration when determining hourly fees is whether the fraud investigation practice will have a single fee structure for all engagements, or whether there will be different fee levels depending on the types of clients, the specifics of a case, and the expertise involved. Some forensic accountants and fraud investigators are strongly opposed to having different fees for different types of projects. Others recognize that discounted rates may be the norm in certain industries, but they do not want to offer those same low rates to all other clients. It is really a matter of finding what works for your firm and your potential clients.

One variation on the hourly fee is a daily or weekly rate for consulting services. Typically, these rates are based on some sort of hourly rate and an estimate of the number of hours per day or week that will be devoted to the project. There does not seem to be much benefit to this rate structure versus hourly rates, but if a firm is more comfortable using this billing method, there does not seem to be any harm in it.

Hourly fees are easy to understand and commonplace among professionals, but that does not mean this is the best way to approach a fraud investigation. Is a forensic accountant or fraud investigator selling her or his time? Or is she or he instead selling expertise? The major argument against using hourly rates is the desire to sell expertise rather than time. When it comes down to it, clients are really buying the expertise of a fraud examiner. Hourly fees are easily manipulated, and hourly rates mean little in a world in which the range of rates can be huge. If you are someone who hates tracking time (especially in tenths of hours), you have another reason to shy away from hourly fees.

Fixed fees are not widely used by accountants, attorneys, and fraud investigators, but they are one way for the professional to charge for the expertise brought to the table. A fixed fee works best when the investigator has done enough upfront work to be able to accurately assess the scope of work to be done and the documentation and resources available. Fixed fees can be tricky to determine unless you have substantial experience investigating fraud. Until the engagement manager has enough experience, it might be better to go the hourly fee route, because with a flat fee there is always a risk that much more time and effort will be involved than the client has paid for. Hourly fees ensure that the investigation team gets compensated for all of its time, and that may be an important goal, especially for a new practice.

A fixed fee should take into account not only the time the investigation team will devote to the project, but also special expertise brought to the engagement, availability of other professionals to do the same work, and details regarding the complexity of the project. Are there things about the engagement that make the investigator's results more valuable? If so, the investigator should charge more for the work.

For example, there may not be a lot of forensic accountants with expertise and experience in securities fraud matters. Therefore, an investigator with such expertise can and should get paid more for this specialized offering. A case may require certain international connections, and that, too, might merit a higher fee. A specialty in criminal tax fraud or certain white-collar crimes like money laundering might mean a greater fee as well. An extremely tight deadline requiring some round-the-clock work should also merit greater compensation.

The objective is not to charge clients as much as possible. But it is fair for a forensic accountant or fraud investigator who brings something special to the table to be well compensated for that. If you have special expertise or there is high demand with little supply of skills like yours, you deserve to be paid for it. If a client is demanding an accelerated work schedule and asking the firm to set aside other projects in favor of their project, that should be compensated, too.

So how does an engagement manager go about developing the fixed fee for a project? One method is to start with a time budget, just as you would on any traditional engagement. Figure out the time commitment, offering your team some room for error on estimating the time, as well as including some time for unexpected work. Factor into the fee the specialized experience discussed previously, as well as your assessment of the value of your work to the business or legal matter. For example, if $25 million is on the line, do you think that your investigation and expert report are worth a certain amount to the case?

Those who have used fixed fees in the past will tell you "yes." A newer fraud investigator might not have a sense of what that value is. More experienced professionals likely have a better handle on the value that their work brings to the case. Here is an excellent example: A longtime client needed a particular calculation done with a one-page summary of the results of that calculation, and he needed it that afternoon. He and I both knew that it would take me only about an hour to put it together. We also both knew that the case could not proceed without this document.

The work could be done in an hour because of my past experience with the issue and familiarity with the case. Was that work worth only one hour of fees? Or was there a higher value because my experience allowed me to do it so quickly, I was willing to drop everything for this client, and the results were critical to the case proceeding? The client and I agreed that the work was worth far more than one billed hour, and we agreed upon a fair fixed fee that reflected the value of that one-page summary to his case.

The obvious objection to the use of fixed fees is the concern that work may be far more extensive than planned, and the fraud investigation team will not be compensated for all of the time they devote to the project. That is a legitimate concern, especially for a firm and project manager who have always billed by the hour. It's especially of concern on larger engagements, which could go on for months or years. The best way to manage a case in this instance is to use *phases*. An experienced lead investigator should be able to break the engagement into pieces, which makes it easier to determine fees.

For example, in a typical embezzlement by an accounting manager, the phases might include:

1. Analysis of financial statements to determine at-risk accounts and departments
2. Detailed examination of at-risk accounts identified in phase one, including analysis of bank statements and supporting documentation
3. Reconstruction of financial statements based upon evidence uncovered and confirmation of actual revenues and expenses
4. Issuance of a report and supporting documentation

This is a rudimentary example, but it is necessary to show how an engagement can be broken into logical pieces in order to aid in the determination of fixed fees.

There are two ways to approach the fixed fee once an engagement is broken into phases. The first is to assign fees to each phase of the engagement immediately. The second is to assign a fee to the first one or two phases, and wait to determine fees for later phases. This would be preferable if the amount of work for the later phases is uncertain, especially if the scope of that work will vary based on findings in earlier phases. The phases are often presented to a client with a recommendation to start on the first few phases and wait to decide on the later phases. Often it's unclear whether those phases will make economic sense until we know more (and we will not know more until we get into the work of the earlier phases).

The key is allowing the client enough flexibility under the fee arrangement so that they feel they are getting the best value. I do not mind waiting to see whether later phases make sense. My job is not to take as much money as possible from the client, especially when later work might not be beneficial to the client. I would rather wait and see and let them make a financial decision once we know more.

Contingency fees are not usually the best way to go when investigating fraud. One of the keys to being an effective fraud investigator is being objective and independent. It is difficult to be independent when the investigator's fees depend on how much fraud is found. It is easy to see how an attorney on the other side of the issue could suggest that the fraud investigator had a financial incentive to inflate the fraud findings. ·

Billing Practices

Collecting fees is another area of engagement administration that can be tenuous. No professional likes to work for free, so collecting fees is an important part of the process. Many fraud investigators require a deposit or retainer up front. In cases that are billed hourly, the future bills are typically offset with that retainer. Once the deposit or retainer has been earned by the firm, there are two options:

1. Bill the client for fees incurred, and wait for payment from the client
2. Request another deposit from the client, with future invoices to be offset against that deposit

The advantage to collecting a deposit before completing more work is that the firm is assured of being paid for all work. The downside is that work may have to be suspended until a deposit is received, and that can disrupt the flow of the investigation.

If a firm is willing to bill a client for fraud investigation services and wait for payment, the payment terms should be very carefully outlined before the start of work. The client should also be made aware that nonpayment of invoices could be cause for the investigation to stop, and this could impact the completion of further work.

Collection of fees in fixed-fee engagements is often a bit easier. If the fee for the engagement (or the current phase of the engagement) is known before work starts, it is easy to make a payment schedule. Some fraud examiners require 25% or 50% of the fees up front, with the remainder to be paid on a certain schedule. In some cases, it might even be appropriate to collect 100% of the fees up front, especially if there is reasonable danger of not being paid in the future.

Criminal defense cases are a good example of the type of case that may warrant 100% of the fees to be paid before work is started. What happens if the fraud investigator performs all of the work, and the findings are not helpful to the defendant? What are the chances that all fees will not be paid? Up front payment will help avoid a situation like this from occurring.

Many forensic accountants and fraud investigators seem to be reluctant to be aggressive about collecting fees, especially when the practice is new and the professionals are trying to establish themselves. There is no good reason, however, to work for free. The fraud investigator provides a valuable service that should be compensated, and there is nothing wrong with taking precautions to ensure that payment is received.

One good way to ensure payment is to specify in the engagement letter that the final report will not be released to the client until all fees have been paid in full. This may sound unusual, but it can be very effective at ensuring payment.

Engagement Letters

An engagement letter is an important document that protects both the client and the fraud investigator. At a minimum, the engagement letter should outline the following:

- *Work to be done.* The amount of detail here will vary depending on the needs of the parties. Sometimes there are very specific parameters and documentation, and in that case it may be easy to be specific about the work being done. Other times, the parties may not be sure what documentation will be available or even how in-depth the work will get. In that case, it is more appropriate to have a loosely worded description of the work.

- *Changes to scope of work.* It should be clear that if the client decides to change the scope of work to be done, the engagement will be suspended until a revised engagement agreement can be made. It's important that the fraud investigator be protected from the client who wants to expand the scope of work without sufficient time or payment of fees. This also helps protect the fraud investigator if the client is trying to lead the investigation in an objectionable direction.
- *Responsibilities of parties.* If the work of the fraud investigator depends on the client to complete certain tasks or provide documentation, this should be clearly stated. For example, it might be a good idea to state that the client is responsible for contacting any outside parties to obtain documentation related to the matter. If the investigation requires copies of invoices from vendors, it is probably much easier for the client to get those than for the investigator to attempt to prove to the vendor that the client has agreed to have the documents released. There is not just one right way to handle the collection of documentation, but it is important that the responsibilities be carefully outlined.
- *Important deadlines.* If there are firm deadlines for the completion of work, these should be laid out in the engagement letter. There might also be contingencies attached to these deadlines. For example, the investigator might state that work is expected to be completed within 90 days, but that depends on timely production of documents by the client. It might even be wise to set dates by which the client must produce documents or complete tasks in order for the ultimate deadline to be met. This is especially important if deadlines are related to court activity. If the court has specified a date by which an expert report must be filed, but the client has not cooperated in a way that will allow the expert to finish the report, what happens? Obviously, the client's case will be in jeopardy, so it is necessary that the fraud investigator protect herself or himself from such problems.

- *Fees and payment terms.* Whether fees are being billed on an hourly or fixed basis, it is important to outline that in the engagement letter. If there are budgets or limits in place, those should be defined. Deposits or retainers should be made clear, and in the event that an engagement is terminated midway through the investigation, it should be clear how fees and deposits will be reconciled.
- *Termination of the engagement.* If the fraud investigator intends to terminate an engagement for nonpayment of fees, deception by the client, conflict of interest, noncooperation by the client, or any other potential problems, it should be clear how that will be handled and what the rights and responsibilities of all parties are.
- *Start of work.* State what must happen before you will start work. Does the client need to sign the engagement agreement? Does a deposit signify a client's agreement with the terms of the engagement and authorize you to start work? Is a verbal agreement sufficient for you to move forward with your investigation?

The ideal engagement agreement is often developed over a period of years and after experience with clients. Unfortunately, negative experiences with clients usually cause the fraud investigator to add clauses to the engagement letter. The professional realizes that she or he has not addressed a particular problem or concern in an engagement letter and adds appropriate verbiage to future letters.

It is not a bad idea to have your attorney look over your standard engagement agreement to ask for input. Some professionals purposely strive to avoid a lot of legalese in their engagement letters. However, the advice of an attorney can still be helpful to ensure that the provisions in your letter are legally enforceable and that you have not missed any key details.

CHAPTER 3

Managing the Case

Fraud investigations may require closer supervision and management than traditional auditing and accounting engagements. A fraud investigation is often time sensitive and dependent on a detailed analysis of a large volume of information. There is usually one chance to get the investigation right. If a case ends up in court, the fraud investigator is relied on to provide a rock-solid expert opinion that can stand up to intense scrutiny.

It should come as no surprise that small investigations and large investigations should be handled differently. Smaller investigations can often easily be handled very informally, especially if only one or two investigators are involved in the project. In contrast, large projects with 10, 20, or more investigators require much more organization, because everyone needs to stay apprised of the status of the case.

Realize that no book on fraud investigations could ever cover all sizes of investigations or types of cases. Instead, I acknowledge that there can be many variations and attempt to address some of the most common issues and solutions. When a fraud investigator encounters a situation that does not fit the parameters of some of the most common circumstances, it is best to consult a highly experienced professional who can help create a strategy.

The focus of this book is on the reactive fraud investigation, which is initiated only after some suspicions of fraud are raised. Proactive investigations (often referred to as ongoing audits of data) are not discussed much, because they are primarily undertaken on a routine basis to search for red flags of fraud, but are not the same thing as fraud investigation started after some sort of evidence of fraud has been uncovered.

Assembling the Team: Where to Start

When a fraud is suspected at a company, the first phone call often goes to an attorney or to a company's auditing or accounting firm. That's the right call to make, but it is important that good decisions be made very quickly about who will ultimately investigate the fraud. Ideally, the lawyer will have experience with fraud and will be able to recommend a qualified fraud investigator for the project.

Management often thinks that the company's accounting or auditing firm should investigate the situation. That makes intuitive sense at first glance, but it is probably not the right decision once management thinks through the consequences. The regular outside auditors or accountants would have a small advantage in a fraud investigation, in that they are already familiar with the company's operations and management. They are probably already aware of some weaknesses in the company's internal controls that might make it easier for an employee to commit fraud. Their familiarity with the company's operations and controls offers an advantage.

But even though the accountants have valuable background information, it does not necessarily mean that they are the right people to investigate allegations of fraud. One issue that can arise is independence. Does the firm have too much of a personal connection with some employees to be neutral during an investigation? Could prior knowledge about employees and the company make them less than objective? Might the firm be too close to the suspect to do a thorough investigation? How would a project like this impact the firm's ability to continue as the independent auditors in the future? It is also possible that the accounting firm's knowledge of the company may cause them to overlook things during an investigation. A separate firm represents a fresh set of eyes, and that can be beneficial when looking for small clues and subtleties.

Management should also inquire about the accounting firm's experience with fraud investigations. Many small firms do not have competent fraud investigators on staff but are willing to engage in this type of work anyway. That is not fair to the client, who deserves to have highly skilled investigators examining allegations of fraud. Management should carefully evaluate the qualifications and credentials of any firm engaged to investigate an internal fraud.

In addition to technical fraud investigation skills, there is also a need for an expert with experience in the court system. Many fraud investigations have the potential to lead to a civil or criminal case. The client should have a fraud examiner who is well versed in expert witness work and has successfully testified in several court cases in the past.

Imagine if a client hired a firm to perform a fraud investigation, and an audit staff member with no real fraud investigation experience was sent to complete the project. Is that fair to the client? What happens if the staff person has no real idea where to start? What if the case ends up in court, and the client finds out the staff member has never testified before? The best firms will never put a client in such a position, and will send inexperienced staff into the field only if they're being closely supervised by a highly qualified fraud investigator.

Assembling the Team: Company Insiders

One common question is whether company insiders should be on the investigation team. If they are on the team, how deeply should they be involved? This question is an excellent one, because one of the chief concerns in a fraud investigation is the objective analysis of facts and evidence. Company insiders sometimes have a hard time looking at a case objectively. The smaller the company, the more likely it is that an employee involved in the investigation would have some personal connection with the accused and the witnesses. This might bring with it some preconceived notions about guilt or innocence. Knowledge about a company's policies and procedures, operating weaknesses, and prior history of disciplining employees (or not) may bias the employee. Even when people have good intentions and they attempt to be objective, that's not always possible.

For small to midsized companies, it is probably best to bring in the independent fraud investigator, and to limit the participation of company insiders. In this type of situation, they would be witnesses of sorts. They should provide information about processes, people, and their observations relative to the suspected fraud. Those who have direct knowledge of the suspected fraud should definitely not participate in the investigation, as they are instead witnesses.

This supportive role of company insiders should not be minimized, however, as it is still critical to a successful fraud investigation. The team will need to rely on insiders to walk them through the systems, help them locate documents and data, and offer their insight about how the fraud might have happened. Without all of this information, the fraud investigator cannot do her or his job effectively.

A management representative and a member of the board of directors should be involved in the investigation as well. They do not have to actually investigate, but management should be aware of the suspicions of fraud and the progress of the investigation. They should also have some input into the direction of the investigation.

Depending on the level of the employee or employees believed to be actively involved in the suspected fraud, the inclusion of a management representative could be a difficult choice. When lower-level employees are suspected of fraud, it is easy to determine that a manager at a level or two above that employee should be apprised of the investigation. That manager is close enough to the suspect to provide valuable information to the fraud investigation team, but hopefully not so close as to compromise the investigation in any way or bring a personal bias to the situation.

The higher the suspected thief is in the company, however, the harder it is to involve management in the investigation. What if the suspect is the company's CEO or CFO? Who would be the right person to be involved with the investigation? A subordinate is probably not the right choice, but who is left? In this case, there may very well not be a management employee who can or should be involved in the investigation. One or more members of the board of directors will have to be involved. The relationship of the board members to the suspect or suspects should be examined as well to try to prevent conflicts of interest or potential biases.

Assembling the Team: Key Participants

A fraud examiner or forensic accountant with experience investigating and analyzing fraud should be in charge of the investigation. As already discussed, each fraud investigation is different, and there is not necessarily a work program or outline that can be followed by an inexperienced investigator. An experienced professional is needed at the helm to ensure that evidence is preserved, all necessary procedures are performed, and that ultimately a thorough investigation is completed.

The right person for this job could have a variety of job titles, possibly including fraud investigator, forensic accountant, fraud examiner, forensic auditor, fraud auditor, special investigator, or private investigator. It is important to look past the title assigned to the professional, and focus instead on the expertise, credentials, and skills that will be relevant to the situation at hand. The larger the case, the more likely there will be several fraud investigators in a role in which they are supervising and managing staff.

Depending on the size of the case, the lead investigator will be accompanied by one or more staff members who are likely less experienced with fraud investigation. Ideally, they will still be able to do independent work, balancing the need for guidance from the lead investigator with a desire to do some on-the-job learning.

Internal or external auditors and accountants can support the investigation with information on company procedures and controls. They can be a resource, and their value to the investigation should not be underestimated. They can likely assist with some of the investigative procedures, if it is determined that they are competent and do not have any apparent conflict of interest. Still, the involvement of these professionals should be limited, particularly as it relates to their investigative skills and their ability to be independent in their work.

Legal counsel must play an active role in the process, often dictating the direction of the investigation. The attorney will have in mind the ultimate conclusion of the situation, and that might include an insurance claim, an internal disciplinary action, a civil lawsuit, or a referral to law enforcement. The intent of the attorney will play a big part in how the investigation is carried out and how much time, effort, and money will be put into the project.

Assembling the Team: Outside Consultants

Outside professionals with particular areas of expertise should be utilized to supplement the skills and experience of the fraud investigator. Some professionals think there is nothing wrong with trying to provide all of the services that a client may need. I would rather provide a client with access to the best professional in a particular area of expertise.

One typical example of this is a computer forensics expert. Companies often discipline employees and secure their company-owned computers. A computer consultant who works with digital evidence for a living is usually the best person to examine those computers and retrieve any evidence. She or he will know how to secure the evidence to make it admissible in court, and will also know about software that can aid in the examination of computers to find deleted or hidden data.

Often, fraud examiners are not private investigators, and it may be necessary to bring in a private investigator for certain aspects of a case. They might have special expertise with asset searches, surveillance, or background checks that could aid the fraud investigator. The key is in knowing and admitting the limitations of your fraud investigation team. Do not compromise a client's investigation by trying to do something you are not qualified to do. It can ruin your reputation and the client's case. It is so much easier to stick to the work for which you have expertise and refer out the other tasks.

Importance of Credentials

Alert clients are on the lookout for meaningful credentials to help them assess the competence of a fraud investigator. Not all credentials are worth something to the client, as many of them are simply the result of paying a fee and receiving a piece of paper.

In light of this, an obvious selling point for a fraud investigator is well-respected credentials. In the field of fraud investigation, the "gold standard" is the Certified Fraud Examiner (CFE). The credential is earned through an application process and a lengthy exam, including questions in the areas of Fraudulent Financial Transactions, Legal Elements of Fraud, Fraud Investigation, and Criminology and Ethics. Annual continuing education requirements help ensure that a fraud investigator is keeping her or his knowledge on fraud detection, prevention, and deterrence current.

The Certified Public Accountant (CPA) credential can also give the client a level of confidence about the fraud investigator's knowledge of finance and accounting concepts. There are plenty of good fraud investigators who do not have this credential, but it is yet one more way to measure the credentials of a professional.

Some fraud investigators are also licensed private investigators. This is not a necessity for fraud examiners and investigators, but it can be helpful when contemplating certain investigative techniques that require licensing. For example, some states require a private investigator's license in order to engage in surveillance.

There are many more certifications available to professionals, but before a client assumes that a credential is evidence of competence, the client should research what the credential really means. Is it one that requires holders to demonstrate their expertise? Or is it merely a credential that can be bought and sold? It is in the client's best interest to be skeptical of credentials, especially ones that do not appear to be mainstream.

Management and Supervision of Staff

The lead investigator should define areas of responsibility in the investigation, making it clear to everyone who is supervising them and to whom they report. There needs to be one central point of contact for all investigative work, and that should obviously be the lead investigator, who will devise the investigation plan, assign responsibilities, monitor work, provide guidance on investigative techniques, gather results, and oversee the final report.

The fraud investigator in charge of the engagement should be in close contact with the attorney advising the client on the fraud matter. It is important that the fraud investigation be conducted in a way that is consistent with the intended direction of the case from a legal standpoint. For example, if the attorney intends to file a civil suit against the perpetrator, the investigation would be much different than if the company simply wanted to investigate to find out what happened in general and to close major holes in the company's internal controls.

The lead investigator will map out what needs to be accomplished and divide the work into areas of focus. The areas could be divided by geographic locations, parties implicated in the fraud, or any other logical division. Depending on the size of the engagement, there may be mid-level supervisors of staff who will each be responsible for one or more areas of investigation. Mid-level supervisors are more likely to be involved in an investigation that has multiple geographic locations or many lengthy phases to the investigation.

Supervisors will help map out work for each area and instruct subordinates on the work they are going to be completing. They will see that the work plan is carried out, approve deviations from the plan, and help solve problems that arise during the engagement. As work is completed, supervisors should determine whether the conclusions and results of work are supported by the evidence. Accuracy should be checked, and staff investigators should be prepared to answer questions about the work they completed and the conclusions they drew. Supervision of staff should be aimed at making sure good evidence-handling procedures are utilized, and that investigation techniques are completed thoroughly.

The work and the results should be critically evaluated. If you were on the opposite side of the case, what would you attack? What questions would arise? What problems or inconsistencies are there? What areas of the case are weak? Where should more evidence be gathered? Ultimately, the lead investigator will be relying on the work of subordinates while testifying in deposition and court. It is imperative that quality control procedures be in place to verify that the conclusions of the investigators are supported by evidence.

As discussed in Chapter 1, the lack of standard work programs in fraud investigations may make closer supervision necessary. Young, inexperienced auditors can rely on work programs to guide their work and instruct them on the required procedures. Without such a tool in a fraud investigation, direct supervision will be more important. There is no magic way to supervise staff on a fraud investigation engagement. As with most professional engagements, less experienced staff will need more guidance in their work. The more experienced your investigators, the less you have to watch over them, and the more you can count on them working competently and asking questions when necessary.

Work Programs and Checklists

As discussed in Chapter 1, one advantage traditional auditors have over fraud investigators is the use of work programs to guide the engagement. Because audits are fairly standardized, the work programs ensure that all critical work is completed, all important questions have been answered, and all key concerns are documented.

Fraud investigators have very little that resembles work programs or investigation guides. Each investigation is unique, which makes it difficult to create a one-size-fits-all approach to performing the engagement. Fraud investigators are more likely to rely on some basic checklists to guide the engagement in general, with specific investigation procedures being developed and performed as the engagement progresses.

Because there are fewer guides for fraud investigators, less experienced staff members probably need closer supervision than regular auditors. While a young auditor can refer to the prior year's audit work papers and work programs to guide her or him through the process, the young investigator is not so lucky.

Unless you've worked in a traditional auditing role, it may be difficult to comprehend just how heavily staff relies on the work programs and the prior year's work papers. Quite simply, probably 85% to 90% of the auditor's work will be done in accordance with them. The remaining 10% to 15% of the work will be based on situations that arise during the audit, such as new company functions or accounting processes, problems found during testing of accounts, new accounting or auditing standards, and new procedures designed to address new risks identified.

Relevant checklists to assist in fraud investigations are developed over time as a fraud investigator gains more experience in the field. The checklists will vary depending on whether the firm works on specific types of cases or in specific industries. There is no one-size-fits-all set of checklists that will help fraud investigators across the board because of the varying types of cases. Fraud investigators will usually develop their own checklists as they gain more experience in the field, but the Appendix has some sample checklists that may provide guidance on developing your own.

Document Management

One of the most basic, yet one of the most important, parts of a fraud investigation is the proper management of documents, both paper and digital. The larger a case gets, the more critical this aspect becomes. Imagine testifying in court and being asked whether you saw a particular document. How would the judge and jury react if you didn't know whether you had seen it, much less considered it in your analysis? Then consider the reaction if you are able to refer to a document inventory and quickly respond that you had seen it, whom you received it from, and how it was integrated into your analysis. Clearly, the latter is more likely to cast the fraud investigator in a positive light.

Certain principles of document management apply equally to small and large cases. First, it is important to know who gave you a document and when you received it. If a document is an original, safeguard it and preserve the chain of custody (discussed in more detail in the next section). Make the most frequently used documents easy to find, so you do not waste time searching for them each time you need to refer to them.

The choices for logging documents (creating an inventory of the documents) range from low- to high-tech. In a very small fraud investigation, there is nothing wrong with keeping a handwritten sheet for your document log. The larger the case, the more likely that you will get a little more high-tech with your process.

Those who prefer computerized document logs may use a spreadsheet or a database to record the receipt of documents. However you choose to do it, the most important information to log is the date the document was received, who produced the document, and a short identifying name for the document. You may also want to log a short description of the document and to whom or what the document relates. See the Appendix for a sample document inventory report. For example, if your investigation includes five business entities, it might be important to log which entity this document relates to. Similarly, if you have multiple suspects or witnesses in a case, you may want to note to which person the document relates.

The larger the case, the more sophisticated the software you will probably use to track the documents. Commercially available software packages can help you track documents, as well as analyze the data and relationships included in those documents.

Documents that arrive prenumbered can make document management a little easier. Lawyers are fond of Bates stamping, so that documents are easily identifiable during the litigation process. Bates stamping is a process by which all documents in a case are assigned a number or a series of letters and numbers to identify them. The assignment of numbers or letters is not standardized, but typically the attorneys will decide to stamp the documents with letters that identify the source of the documents and then sequential numbers. So, for example, documents produced by defendant Ann Davis might be numbered: AD 0001, AD 0002, AD 0003, and so on.

Make sure you are clear on how the documents in a particular case have been Bates stamped. You need to know whether the letters or numbers have any specific meaning. The Bates-stamped numbers are helpful during an investigation, especially if the universe of documents includes several versions of a similar document. It is easy to identify a document that has a Bates number, so that all parties can be assured that they are examining exactly the same version of a document that you have mentioned in your report. Do not forget to log the corresponding Bates-stamped numbers when creating the document inventory.

Remember that documentation includes computerized documents as well. You might be provided with a piece of computer media that holds 5,000 scanned documents related to the case. It will be important to go through those documents and log relevant information about them, too. If investigators are lucky, they will be provided with an index of all documents on the media. This is not a substitute for examining the documents, however. It is still important to look through them and determine whether they will play a role in your analysis.

A "key documents file" can make it easier to work with documents in a case, especially if a small number of documents need to be referred to frequently. This is another low-tech way of organizing things in your investigation. It is recommended that you leave the original copy of the document in with all of the other documents, sorted appropriately within your organization scheme. Take a copy of the document, and keep it in your key documents file for quick reference. Items that might be good candidates for the key documents file are real estate closing statements, key months of bank statements, a chart of accounts, or other pieces of evidence that you will be referencing frequently.

Preserving Evidence

Part of the document management process is preserving original evidence so that it may someday be used in court. While an investigator often does not know whether a case will ultimately end up in front of a judge, the most prudent way to handle evidence is to assume that you will be in court one day and to handle the evidence carefully.

Digital evidence is relatively easy to preserve if you use the help of a knowledgeable professional. Your best bet is to bring in an expert in computer forensics, preferably someone who has testified in court several times. That person is most likely to properly preserve digital evidence for later presentation in court.

At all costs, do not allow anyone to do anything to the computers used by the suspect(s) in the fraud case. The mere act of looking through computer files can destroy important data and can compromise the integrity of the digital evidence. Even turning a computer on or off makes changes to its hard drive, which could later call into question the evidence. Allow only a qualified computer forensics expert to touch the computers in question.

Documentary evidence will need to be preserved, too, and the investigator will have to demonstrate a proper chain of custody of the evidence if the matter ends up in court. Chain of custody is a fancy way of saying that it is important to secure evidence and demonstrate that it was not tampered with or altered. You will have to show who had access to the evidence, how it was secured, and how its integrity was preserved.

If you are put in charge of a piece of evidence, it is best for you to lock it in a cabinet and/or office that has very limited access. You should know exactly who has keys to the room or storage device. If you need to move the evidence or give it to someone, you should have documentation prepared relative to that transfer of evidence, and the person receiving it should be prepared to keep it secure and document its whereabouts as well.

Investigators should not write on originals in any way or otherwise destroy or mark them. Make copies of the originals, and use the copies as your working documents for the investigation if you need to write on them or otherwise mark them. Do your best to keep the original evidence in exactly the same condition in which it was received. If you receive only copies of evidence, you do not have to worry about preserving it carefully. After all, it is not the actual evidence.

The process of preserving evidence is especially important in cases in which the suspect is alleging that evidence has been altered, signatures are not authentic, or documents are forged or fabricated. As a general rule of thumb, make sure originals of all documents are secured and their chain of custody is documented.

Sometimes when a fraud investigator is called in, the integrity of some evidence has already been compromised. That is not the investigator's fault, and the status of the evidence should be carefully documented so that the investigator doesn't later get blamed for this situation.

File Maintenance

It is important for all members of the fraud investigation team to understand and apply good file maintenance procedures. Particularly in cases that may escalate to litigation, rules should be followed by the fraud investigators (expert witnesses for litigation purposes) to ensure that the expert's report and testimony are not tainted.

Anything that was used to help form an opinion in the case should be kept with the file. The fraud investigator may need to refer back to that item, and the other side of the case has a right to see it as well. It is not a good idea to haphazardly throw out documents in a case. It is more appropriate to keep everything that was produced for you, and segregate the documents into two sets: items that will be used in your analysis and items that will not be used.

Why wouldn't you use something that was produced by a party to the litigation? Documents are often produced that have no bearing on the fraud investigation. This might include contracts with unrelated parties, personnel files of uninvolved employees, details of transactions that are not relevant to the case, or account statements for customers that are not included in the investigation.

There is no rule of thumb for including or excluding documents from your investigation. An experienced fraud investigator should go through the documents produced and decide which ones need detailed examination on a case-by-case basis. Do not make the mistake of relying on the client's judgment about what you need or do not need. Look at all available documentation related to the matter, and make an independent decision about whether items are relevant.

Note-taking is an important part of any professional's work. There are varying schools of thought on the issue of taking notes during a fraud investigator's discussions, meetings, field work, interviews, and document review. On one end of the spectrum is the advocate for no notes. To this investigator, if there are no notes, there is nothing for opposing counsel to examine if the case ends up in court. While that may sound like a clever strategy, it doesn't seem to make a lot of practical sense. I haven't met anyone who is able to remember everything they ever heard or saw, so notes are a way to refresh one's memory during an investigation. No notes also make it difficult for team members to evaluate what others have done or seen in a case. The absence of notes imposes limitations on the staff that are not practical or helpful.

On the other end of the spectrum is the investigator who believes everything should be written in the notes. Even one tiny detail should not be lost if proper notes are kept of everything. The problem with that is that in the case of litigation, all those notes will eventually be discoverable by opposing counsel. Your working theories or lines of thinking will be exposed, and any preliminary conclusions you may have written about will be open to scrutiny. I prefer a moderate approach, leaning toward the "less is more" theory. A fraud investigator should take modest notes on facts only, noting details that might become important to the investigation. It is appropriate to make notes about who is responsible for certain functions in a company, how the work flows, dollar figures in question, and what the procedures are.

Avoid notes that may embarrass you later. You do not need to make notes about anyone's appearance or demeanor. If someone was rude, you will remember that. There is no need to put it in your notes and potentially give rise to a later claim that you are biased or had a negative attitude toward someone. Avoid writing about preliminary opinions in your notes, or about your initial impressions on guilt or innocence. Take a "just the facts" approach to note-taking, and there will be less to criticize later. Make sure your notes include dates of meetings and who was present and providing key information. With this fact-based approach, you will have the important points on paper in case you need to refer to them, but you do not have anything that calls your opinions and independence into question.

As will be discussed in Chapter 11, it might be necessary to disclose in your report what documents you relied on in forming your opinion. Good file maintenance practices will help this process as well.

Investigative Software

Several software packages are available to assist fraud investigators with tracking documents, analyzing relationships between people and entities, and identifying vulnerabilities in a company's controls; however, a fraud investigator's skills are ultimately what will make an investigation successful. Fancy software cannot make up for a lack of technical skills or investigative intuition. Software might help someone with poor organizational skills to better track documents and work flow, but there are inherent limitations to software that require a skilled investigator.

Some great fraud investigations have been completed without the assistance of investigation software. A thorough and competent investigation can easily be complete without such a tool. Many fraud investigators will even suggest that a low-tech approach to investigating produces even better results. A software package is probably most helpful when it comes to analyzing large quantities of data, looking for unusual relationships between numbers or unexpected changes in account balances. If software has identified questionable transactions or parties to a transaction, an investigator will need to examine the items identified to determine whether they need further analysis.

Much of a fraud investigation still involves combing through records, either in hardcopy or in digital format, verifying and cross-checking information. Experienced fraud investigators agree that much can be done with pen, paper, and a calculator. Spreadsheets and databases can help the investigator extract and track certain data, and then summarize and manipulate that data to draw conclusions.

Professional Standards

Depending on an investigator's professional licensing and membership in professional organizations, the standards that apply to investigative work will vary. It is easy to say that a professional fraud investigator should be thorough and exercise due professional care. It is another to know the requirements of your organization and licensing body.

If the fraud investigator is a Certified Public Accountant, the professional standards issued by the American Institute of Certified Public Accountants (AICPA) require that the professional follow *Statement on Standards for Consulting Services No. 1*. In general, the CPA must:

- Exhibit professional competence, performing only engagements that she or he (and the firm) can complete competently.
- Use due professional care in performing the engagement.
- Adequately plan and supervise the engagement.
- Obtain sufficient relevant data that can provide a reasonable basis for the professional's conclusions.
- Meet the objectives of the engagement with the client while maintaining integrity and objectivity.
- Have a written or oral understanding with the client about the responsibilities of each party and the scope of the engagement.
- Inform the client when there is a conflict of interest, when the CPA has reservations about the scope of the engagement, and of significant findings during the engagement.

It should be clear that, unlike audit engagements, fraud investigation engagements do not require independence on the part of the accountant. Instead, the fraud investigation requires only objectivity to be exercised.

If the fraud investigator is a member of the Association of Certified Fraud Examiners (ACFE), she or he is required to abide by the Standards of Professional Conduct. The standards require the professional to:

- Conduct the engagement with integrity.
- Disclose potential conflicts of interest to the client.
- Maintain objectivity during the engagement.
- Conduct herself or himself in the best interest of the reputation of the profession.

- Not knowingly make false statements when testifying.
- Comply with lawful orders of the court.
- Not commit criminal acts or knowingly induce others to do so.
- Be competent in the engagements accepted.
- Comply with continuing education requirements of the organization.
- Exercise due professional care in performance of the engagement.
- Make conclusions that are supported by sufficient, relevant, and competent evidence.
- Adequately plan the engagement.
- Adequately supervise assistants.
- Reach an agreement with the client about the scope of the engagement.
- Communicate significant findings to the client.
- Not disclose confidential or privileged information obtained during the course of the investigation, except with proper permission.
- Conduct fraud examinations in a legal, professional, and thorough manner to obtain complete, reliable, and relevant evidence.
- Establish predication and scope priorities and be efficient in her or his work.
- Consider potential bias of witnesses, as well as exculpatory and inculpatory evidence.
- Preserve the integrity of evidence and the chain of custody.
- Gather documentation in accordance with the needs and objectives of the client.
- Provide a report that is not misleading and contains only opinions that are based upon sufficient, relevant data within the member's area of expertise.
- Not give an opinion on the legal guilt or innocence of any person or party.

Private investigator licensing rules vary from state to state, so a fraud investigator who is also a licensed private investigator should follow her or his state's rules. There are many other professional organizations for fraud investigators, so obviously the fraud examiner should follow any standard put in place by them.

To some professionals, the number of standards that the fraud investigator must consider is high. An alternative view is that a fraud investigator should quite simply be competent in the profession, have sufficient data and evidence to support the opinions, and be as objective as possible in performing the engagement. It is really quite that simple.

When to Stop Investigating

How does a fraud investigator know when enough investigation has been done on a case? If the scope of work was agreed upon with the client, the investigator should finish that work in order to meet her or his obligations. However, there could come a point in the investigation when the cost outweighs the benefit of further investigation. The client relies on the fraud investigator's expertise and experience to guide the work. It is not the investigator's job to spend as much of the client's money as possible or stretch out the engagement as long as possible.

The fraud investigator should alert the client to the issue, and explain why there may not be much benefit in continuing the investigation. If the client still decides to continue the work, the fraud examiner should cooperate. Ultimately, it is the client's decision to continue or suspend work.

The client is relying on the experience and expertise of the fraud investigator to guide them through the process of investigating. A good fraud investigator makes reasonable recommendations throughout the work, keeping in mind the best interest of the client and the costs related to continued investigation. Clients appreciate the investigator who is willing to advise them that continuing investigation makes no sense, as well as the investigator who describes the reasons why continued investigation will likely be beneficial. Be willing to make a reasonable recommendation to the client, who is relying on your professional judgment about the direction of the investigation.

CHAPTER 4

Searching for Fraud

If a specific instance of fraud has been identified, that will dictate which financial statement accounts are examined by the fraud investigation team in detail. But what if no conclusive evidence of fraud exists, and the investigator is instead looking for clues that might point to a fraud? The company has become suspicious, yet has little hard proof that anything unusual has occurred.

In that case, the investigator must dig through at-risk accounts and functions to look for suspicious activity. Analysis of the financial statements will provide clues about the potential for fraud. Ratios may look unusual. Account balances may be out of line with recent history. Key documentation may be missing. These types of red flags will point the investigator toward areas that deserve additional investigation.

Those not familiar with beginning an investigation with an analysis of the financial statements may not believe this is truly effective in pinpointing areas that are vulnerable to fraud. But inevitably, whenever there is a fraud, something has been overlooked by the fraudster. No matter how well she or he tries to cover their tracks, telltale signs are always left behind.

The more clever the fraudster, the smaller and less detectable those clues will be. But make no mistake, they will be there. That is just the nature of fraud. Unusual activity creates unusual patterns in the numbers and affects key financial ratios. It would be next to impossible for a fraudster to anticipate all of these signs and compensate for them.

Digging into the numbers could be done digitally (with the assistance of software) or manually, depending on the sophistication of the company's records and the auditing software available to the investigator. With large volumes of data to analyze, the benefits of software are obvious. It can quickly analyze thousands of numbers and return results of a much smaller magnitude for further analysis by the fraud investigator.

Analytical Review

Ratio analysis and analytical review procedures are very familiar techniques for financial statement auditors. While analytical procedures may seem elementary, they can be very important in giving clues to areas of the financial statements that may contain fraud. Analytical review involves comparing changes in numbers between accounting periods (horizontal analysis) and the relationships between certain financial statement line items (vertical analysis). The numbers for a business typically have certain predictable patterns, and when the financial results fall outside those parameters, it may be cause for concern.

Typical sets of data to be compared during analytical review can include:

- *Current-period figures versus prior-period numbers.* Commonly, this year is compared to last year, and potentially also years before that.
- *Actual financial results compared to budgeted or projected figures compiled before that accounting period.* How do actual results compare to management's estimates before the accounting period?
- *Company data compared to operational facts.* For example, if production went up, did revenue and accounts receivable increase by reasonable amounts?
- *Company data compared to industry data.* Look for unusual deviations from similar companies, potentially indicating fraud or manipulation of financial statements. For example, a company that has much higher

profitability than similarly situated companies in the industry might be cause for concern.

- *Numerical data compared to notes to the financial statement.* Do the explanations in the notes and the actual numbers make sense?

Vertical analysis should be completed with respect to line items on the financial statement as a percentage of other line items. One typically predictable relationship occurs between revenue and cost of goods sold. A business will have a normal percentage of cost of goods sold to revenue. Some financial statement line items rise and fall in relation to revenue, and those patterns should be examined carefully. Balance sheet items are analyzed in this way as well, often by comparing liabilities and assets, comparing certain assets to total assets, and so on.

Period-to-period changes should also be examined via a horizontal analysis, and the dollars should be compared, as well as the percentage change between periods. Any significant jump in either of these figures should merit further scrutiny. When doing an analysis like this, the fraud investigator should turn up a normal level of professional skepticism. She or he should be specifically looking for things that don't make sense or that represent an unusual change or shift. Of course, there are normal variations in numbers in any business, and that should be considered when analyzing the financial statements. In this analysis, items that fall outside normal variances should be emphasized.

Key Financial Ratios

Financial ratios should be examined as a part of the analytical review procedures. Some of the ratios that are more likely to be affected by a fraud from within include asset turnover, inventory turnover, accounts receivable turnover, debt to equity, gross margin, operating margin, and profit margin. The following are some of the ratios that may aid in uncovering areas of concern in a company's financial statement. It is not meant to be an exhaustive list. Rather, it is a starting point in searching for fraud.

Ratios Related to Sales

Ratios related to sales can be some of the most important figures to analyze. One of the highest-risk areas of the financial statements is revenue, and it is the most likely to be inflated. If sales are really increasing at a company, certain other accounts should be moving in relation to that. If those account balances are not changing in this predictable fashion, the potential that fraudulent revenue is being booked is higher. Sales should ideally be compared to cost of goods sold, gross profit, accounts receivable, sales commissions, returns and allowances, and direct labor costs.

The gross profit percentage is often predictable in companies. Any significant changes should be cause for concern. There should also be concern when evidence indicates that market conditions are changing in ways that should impact this ratio, yet it remains unchanged.

$$\text{Gross Profit Percentage} = \frac{\text{Gross Profit}}{\text{Net Sales}}$$

Fraudulently inflating sales usually requires that the recorded sales are reversed at some later date. If it is recorded as a return by a customer, this could throw the sales return percentage out of line with historical numbers.

$$\text{Sales Return Percentage} = \frac{\text{Sales Returns}}{\text{Total Sales}}$$

Ratios Related to Assets

Asset-related ratios can point to fraud problems, sometimes in ways in which the fraud perpetrator did not expect. One typical problem when a company is fraudulently inflating revenues and earnings is that the company's cash position suffers. There appear to be profits, yet they never seem to turn into positive cash flow. An analysis of the cash position of the company might point to this problem.

With each of the following ratios, the fraud investigator should be looking for unusual relationships. For example, the current ratio or quick ratio has spiked up, possibly indicating that management has falsely inflated the current assets in order to create a base against which the company can borrow more money from the bank.

$$\text{Current Ratio} = \frac{\text{Current Assets}}{\text{Current Liabilities}}$$

$$\text{Quick Ratio} = \frac{\text{Current Assets Less Inventory}}{\text{Current Liabilities}}$$

Ratios Related to Accounts Receivable

Falsely inflating revenue often produces unusual results in accounts receivable, because that is usually the account that is used in conjunction with false entries to revenue accounts. Potential fraud can be identified when there is a sudden unusual change in these ratios.

$$\text{Accounts Receivable Turnover} = \frac{\text{Sales}}{\text{Average Accounts Receivable}}$$

$$\text{Days in Receivables} = \frac{365}{\text{Receivable Turnover}}$$

$$\text{Receivable Percentage} = \frac{\text{Accounts Receivable}}{\text{Total Assets}}$$

A simple analysis of bad debts can point to fraud problems, as fraudulently recorded sales usually lead to phony accounts receivable that need to be removed from the books at some point. Doing so can create a situation in which bad debt expense shows an unusual spike.

$$\text{Bad Debt Percentage} = \frac{\text{Bad Debt Expense}}{\text{Average Accounts Receivable}}$$

$$\text{Bad Debt Percentage} = \frac{\text{Bad Debt Expense}}{\text{Total Sales}}$$

Ratios Related to Inventory

Manipulation of sales numbers and inventory balances can sometimes be spotted in an analysis of inventory. Booking fraudulent sales often leads to false entries to inventory accounts as well, because it is usually necessary to fraudulently manipulate cost of goods sold in conjunction with the revenue manipulation. At some point, the inventory numbers may need to be adjusted because of the fraud, and that may be reflected with unusual ratios.

Inventory schemes and purchasing schemes can also affect the inventory ratios. For example, the inventory turnover ratio could be unusually high if there is a theft of inventory (which causes the company to recognize a higher cost of goods sold). The average days in inventory ratio can give clues about purchasing schemes that create fictitious inventory and cause an increase in this ratio.

$$\text{Average Days in Inventory} = \frac{365}{\text{Inventory Turnover}}$$

$$\text{Inventory Turnover} = \frac{\text{Cost of Goods Sold}}{\text{Average Inventory}}$$

$$\text{Inventory Percentage} = \frac{\text{Inventory}}{\text{Total Assets}}$$

Ratios Related to Liabilities

Schemes to manipulate the financial statements are often aimed at increasing assets while decreasing the liabilities, in order to make the company's financial position look stronger. This can sometimes be discovered by analyzing liabilities, which might be lower than expected because of the fraud.

$$\text{Debt to Equity} = \frac{\text{Total Liabilities}}{\text{Stockholders Equity}}$$

$$\text{Debt Percentage} = \frac{\text{Total Liabilities}}{\text{Total Assets}}$$

When analyzing financial statements and ratios in this manner, there are often simple explanations for the changes between periods or the failure of the predictable patterns on the financial statements. Maybe an employee was hired for a new position, skewing expected payroll numbers. A new marketing initiative can be the catalyst for higher than normal advertising expenses. A radical increase in the cost of raw materials might throw expected ratios out of balance. An inventory control problem might skew the inventory-related ratios.

It is important to rule out obvious explanations for some of the variances found during the analytical review. That does not mean the fraud investigator takes all explanations at face value without any follow-up. Some independent verification of the explanations is often in order.

Ultimately, the purpose of the analytical review is to identify areas of the financial statements that might be affected by fraud. These line items are identified as unusual, without an apparent explanation. This type of work does not prove fraud. It is just a starting point in trying to find clues about a potential fraud. This work can often reveal interesting things when the investigator is following up on identified issues and examining supporting documentation.

The more data can be broken down for the analytical review process, the better the results of the work. Breaking down numbers by division, product, geographic location, or other common sense measure will yield more valuable information. Looking at figures for periods shorter than one year can help, too, as it may offer insight into seasonality of the business. Breaking down numbers prior to doing analytical review will help, because it is not as easy to hide things in these smaller units. Annual figures can easily hide irregular expenses or other line items. Significant increases or decreases are not so easily hidden in monthly or quarterly figures.

Write-offs, Adjustments, and Miscellaneous

In any business, there are certain accounts or areas of the business that carry more risk for suspicious activity. Sometimes it is because the controls are lax, and it is easy for errors and irregularities to flow through the system undetected. Other times it is because employees have become so familiar with the processes and controls that they are able to exploit weaknesses in the system and know that they will likely not be caught.

Accounts with a high volume of low-dollar transactions can be risky, because employees know that the entries to these accounts are likely not examined in detail. There are simply too many individual entries to the account for someone to go through them and verify their validity. That makes such accounts an easy place to "dump" fraudulent trans-actions. Accounts that are used for write-offs, credits, and adjustments are vulnerable to this risk, because they often contain a large number of small entries. Management is notorious for not doing a lot to validate the entries made to these accounts, especially when the individual entries fall below a particular threshold.

It is not unusual for a company to have a specific dollar figure under which no supervisor approval is needed for an employee to adjust or credit an account. Thresholds like this are ripe for abuse by employees, because they can cover a theft of any reasonable size by breaking it down into multiple amounts under this limit, and no one may question the entries.

Management can attempt to head off problems like this by analyzing data for these types of accounts. It is most efficient to use software to perform the analysis, as a large number of transactions can be quickly analyzed. Some of the things that an investigator might be looking for include:

- A higher number of adjustments or write-offs by a particular employee
- An unusually high number of transactions that fall just below the threshold for supervisory approval
- Greater number of round dollar amounts entered as adjustments
- Customer or vendor accounts adjusted more frequently than others

The key to preventing fraud with accounts like this is periodic mon-itoring, at a minimum. Part of the reason why employees utilize these accounts to cover fraud is because they believe no one is scrutinizing them. If a program is put into place to analyze the accounts periodically or continuously, the risk of employee fraud using these accounts immediately goes down.

Manual Disbursements

In the course of conducting business, each company has a procedure (either formally or informally) for disbursing money to vendors. Any disbursement that falls outside of those procedures could be considered a manual disbursement. That is, it is initiated manually and issued under special circumstances.

Probably the most common type of manual disbursement occurs in a company that has an accounts payable process through which all vendor payments should flow. Suppose a vendor drops off materials and needs to be paid immediately for that delivery, and there is not a chance to get the vendor payment through the regular accounts payable process. A check will be cut directly to the vendor, and the accounting system is updated later. This is a classic example of a manual disbursement. It is easy to see how this could occur at any business from time to time. There can be cash-only deliveries, an immediate need for office supplies and an employee willing to go to the store, or a lunch meeting with a food delivery from a restaurant. In each of these cases, it would probably be considered normal for a check to be cut outside of the accounts payable process.

The occurrence of manual disbursements has the potential to create a problem, however. It is an easy way for an employee with access to checks, signature stamps, and other company information to steal funds. The theft could be covered by entering information into the accounting system indicating a cash-only delivery from a supplier. Paperwork might not even be required, because the payment is not going through the accounts payable system. It is only later that someone realizes there is no supporting documentation.

Because this is potentially an easy way to commit fraud, it is important to examine the cash disbursements to see how often manual disbursements are being made and what circumstances surround those payments. It might be helpful to sample some of these disbursements and look for supporting documentation. It is even more important to examine these when the frequency appears very high or otherwise unusual.

At one company, the accounting manager was writing checks to himself but recording manual disbursements to suppliers to balance the bank account and cover the theft. He knew that the company's controls over supplies and inventory were poor, so management would be unable to reconcile amounts on hand to the accounting records. After his theft was uncovered entirely by accident, an examination of the disbursements revealed an unusually high number of manual disbursements. Management knew that cash-only deliveries were rare, so there should not have been this volume of manually issued payments. Had someone examined these types of transactions, the theft likely would have been discovered much sooner.

What about Financial Statement Audits?

Many consumers, investors, professionals, and users of financial statements mistakenly believe that financial statement audits performed by independent accounting firms are akin to fraud investigations. They think that if fraud is present, an audit will find it. After all, what else are they paying for, if not to find fraud?

The financial statement audits done by external auditors are not designed to detect fraud, plain and simple. Audits of financial statements really do two things, when you break them down to the most basic objectives: (1) they double check the math to see whether everything has been added and subtracted correctly; and (2) they make sure that Generally Accepted Accounting Principles (GAAP) have been correctly applied. That may not sound like much, but that is what audits are. Audits were never designed to detect fraud.

Now, you are wondering why audits are not changed so that they become more effective at detecting fraud. That is easier said than done.

The bodies that govern the work of auditors have not done that, and probably will not do it anytime soon. Audits have a specific purpose, and that purpose is largely being fulfilled by the work done by today's auditors. There is no pressure to change that. Even the Sarbanes-Oxley Act, which was intended to make audits more effective and therefore give investors greater confidence in the financial statements of public companies, really has not done much to decrease fraud.

In conjunction with Sarbanes-Oxley, accounting and auditing bodies took some steps to address the issue of fraud. *Statement on Auditing Standards No. 99: Consideration of Fraud in a Financial Statement Audit* was issued in 2002 by the Auditing Standards Board of the American Institute of Certified Public Accountants (AICPA). It became effective for audits of financial statements for periods beginning on or after December 15, 2002. In general, this statement requires auditors to do a little more work regarding the issue of fraud. It does not, however, make auditors responsible for detecting fraud. Auditors are required to:

- Consider the risks and potential for fraud prior to the audit.
- Have a brainstorming session to come up with ways that fraud might be perpetrated and concealed at the company.
- Consider the results of analytical procedures, and determine whether any of them could be indicative of irregularities or fraud.
- Exercise professional skepticism when considering the potential for fraud.
- Inquire with management and key employees to determine whether there have been lapses in internal controls that could lead to fraud.
- Think about the evidence gathered during the audit and decide whether there may be indications that fraud has occurred.

If these points seem insignificant, that is because they largely are. These are, quite frankly, things that auditors should do anyway. Auditors should already be planning engagements in a way that addresses the risk of fraud and misstatements in the financial statements. Information developed during audit planning and performance that suggests fraud might have occurred should be examined further. This standard does nothing more than repeat the auditor's responsibility to do his or her job, yet doesn't really require the detection of fraud. This standard essentially says that if an auditor finds something that might be linked to fraud, it should be dealt with. And if nothing is found, that is okay, too.

These steps have not really protected the users of financial statements from fraud any more than they were protected before. The new standards were largely window dressing, meant to give the general public greater comfort that something was being done. In reality, little has changed. So, to suggest that financial statement audits can negate the need for fraud investigations could not be further from the truth.

Audits have a small place in a company's management of the accounting and financial statement process. They can have a slight deterrent effect when it comes to fraud, because employees who are typically honest will fear that an audit might catch any wrongdoing that they are contemplating. But audits do not directly address fraud, and any company interested in preventing and detecting fraud must do much more than just have an annual audit. They must take proactive steps to both prevent fraud and seek out instances of fraud. Companies must not use audits as their chief fraud prevention and detection effort.

Looking for Fraud in Little Things

What is the difference whether employees are stealing from a company via expense reports? To many people, that seems like a minor thing, not worthy of much consideration. Especially in today's business world, which includes many billion-dollar companies, the idea of worrying about a few hundred dollars' worth of fraud seems silly. Yet these small thefts can be indicators of bigger problems within companies, and that's what makes them so important. Cheating on expense reports is a very typical theft within companies, and it happens with employees at all levels. When companies choose to not crack down on this behavior, however, they are sending a message that some level of unethical behavior is condoned.

In one case, a highly compensated executive systematically cheated on his expense reports. It was common knowledge that he inflated the cost of his cab rides, double expensed meals, and claimed bogus cash expenses like tips. In the grand scheme, he was stealing less than a couple hundred dollars per month this way.

Why would a highly paid executive need to steal such petty amounts? It turns out that is just how he did business in general. His life was built around stealing as much as he could from his employer. His attitude toward expense reporting matched his attitude toward the organization's money in general. He committed a large theft of funds from the organization, and the expense report theft could have tipped someone off to his moral code much earlier.

In terms of dollars lost, expense report theft remains an immaterial item in the financial picture of many companies. But in terms of what this kind of theft might signify about dishonesty in other areas of the company, it is very material. Especially when expense report theft is common knowledge as an accepted practice for a company, it bodes terribly for fraud prevention efforts throughout the organization. There is no such thing as a fraud that is too small, especially when it comes to upper management. Every fraud can be an indicator of big risks and even bigger frauds in areas of the company that might otherwise have been considered secure. Fraud investigators and management must take small frauds seriously.

CHAPTER 5

Sources of Information

Without information, a fraud investigation goes nowhere. There are so many sources of information on people and companies, and as the Internet continues to expand, so does the accessibility of the information. Doing a thorough fraud investigation often goes beyond just analyzing documents that are given to you. The best fraud investigators are able to go beyond those papers and computer files, find additional sources of information, and get legal access to it. There is plenty of art to finding information and clues in an investigation, and it all starts with knowing what to looking for.

Who Acquires Information

It is important to make it clear on the front end of a fraud investigation who will be responsible for acquiring and providing information. Obviously, the client is responsible for producing the documents in its possession, but the fraud investigator needs to determine what the client should produce. Vague requests for information from the client usually will not be very effective in getting the best, most relevant information. The fraud investigator must put together a fairly specific request list and guide the client through interpreting and responding to that request.

It should be clear that there may be additional requests, and that the client should not be afraid to volunteer other information. Hopefully, employees of the client can suggest other items that will aid the investigator, and the investigator can evaluate whether those will indeed be helpful.

If documentation is needed from parties that the client does business with, it is very important to decide who will be responsible for requesting that information. Sometimes copies of invoices, purchase orders, shipping documents, or other items from customers, vendors, or professional service providers can provide very important information to the investigator. Information that comes from a third party can be particularly valuable when investigating an internal fraud, because documents in the possession of outside parties are less likely to be altered or manipulated. Documents from third parties can confirm information about transactions and may also give clues to additional things that should be investigated.

Often, it is easiest for the client to request these items from the third party and direct the provider to send them to the fraud investigator. It is more cumbersome for the fraud investigator to try to get the documents, because the investigator may not know whom to contact or exactly what to ask for. The third party may require a release from the client before it will provide the documents. There are often more steps in the process if the fraud investigator is responsible for getting the documents, which makes this a less desirable option. However, there are times when it may be necessary for the investigator to get these documents directly, especially if there are some suspicions about whether the client might tamper with what is provided.

If the fraud investigator and client agree that the client will be responsible for acquiring certain information from third parties, make sure this agreement is documented clearly. Also make it clear to the client that if they do not (or cannot) get this information, your ability to fully investigate the case may be negatively impacted.

Third-party documentation that will be acquired through the legal process will be the attorney's responsibility. The attorney may request help from the fraud investigator in developing lists of documents to request, and this often helps increase the quality of the information provided. The forensic accountant or fraud investigator should also help inspect documents received to determine whether what was provided is truly responsive to the attorney's requests. It may be necessary to make follow-up document requests.

Information that can be obtained from Internet resources or public databases will most often be acquired by the fraud investigator. After all, that type of detective work is what the client is expecting, and that is an area of expertise for the forensic accountant or fraud investigator.

Internal Records

In a corporate fraud investigation, the most abundant source of information about the fraud will likely come from internal records. Remember that the internal records will be not only paper records but digital as well. The more sophisticated the company, the greater the chance that the bulk of its records will be computerized. Therefore, you will need to work proficiently with digital records.

Typical internal records requested by a fraud investigator include accounting system data, financial statements, tax returns, sales and accounts receivable records, expense documentation, and proof of payments to vendors. The list of things that a fraud investigator could request from the client is endless, so it depends on the specifics of the case. A thorough understanding of accounting is beneficial here, because there is so much to be learned from the client's accounting records, if only the investigator knows what to ask for.

Find contacts within the company who will be able to help you get the documents you need. Management should be able to provide a list of responsible parties for the various areas of the company, and should tell you who will have the greatest familiarity with the documentation. The client should be willing to provide you with complete access to any and all employees needed to complete your investigation. This does not mean that the fraud investigator will monopolize the time of employees and put them to work on lengthy tasks related to the investigation. It does mean that the client must provide reasonable access to the employees who will need to answer questions and gather documentation. If more significant assistance from employees is needed, the client should be willing to work that out with the fraud investigator so that the investigation goals can be accomplished, but the company's normal operations can continue.

The key is to work with the most knowledgeable employees who can help you access the information you need in the most efficient way. Sometimes that literally involves sitting together and walking through reports or computer menus to determine what will provide the information the fraud investigation team needs. Accounting system reports offering the information the investigator needs may be found on a trial-and-error basis, as the right reports are not always the ones used by personnel on a daily basis.

Investigations will not necessarily rely heavily on internal records, because they may often not be available. Consider an investigation of a public company by an outside party. The public company will have certain financial statements and disclosures on file with the Securities and Exchange Commission (SEC), and those will likely be a starting point for an investigation. But that is as close as you may ever get to internal documents until a lawsuit is filed and the company starts producing documents during discovery.

There may also be legitimate reasons why a company does not have internal records to aid in your investigation. A fire or flood may have destroyed the records the forensic accountant is being called in to reconstruct. A malicious employee may have destroyed paper records or computerized data. The company may have an archaic or unreliable system, from which the internal records may be of limited usefulness.

It is clear that internal accounting records and other operational data may play a major role in a fraud investigation. But these records are by no means exhaustive of what a fraud investigator may use during the case. Many more resources are available, as discussed throughout the rest of this chapter.

Private Records

Bank Records

Bank records, including bank statements, canceled checks, and deposit tickets are some of the most useful financial documents in a fraud investigation. Bank records are so valuable because they constitute proof of what actually happened with the money, and the documentation is considered very reliable because it comes from an unaffiliated third party.

Whether in hardcopy or digital format, the bank documentation provides proof positive of how much was paid or received, and to whom it was paid or from whom it was received. In cases in which a company's accounting records have been compromised, these source documents are instrumental to reconstructing the finances and determining definitively where the money went.

Bank documents in a case can create mountains of paper very quickly. The larger the company, the larger the number of bank transactions. Analyzing these documents is obviously time consuming but necessary in cases in which the flow of money is being definitively traced. In addition to the large volume of documents that can be produced by banks, the examination of bank records includes some additional challenges. It may be difficult to identify all active bank accounts, especially if someone suspected of being involved in the fraud has concealed the existence of some accounts.

No database tracks all bank accounts in the name of a person or company, so it is relatively easy to hide a bank account. To get bank records, you have to know which banks to subpoena, and that information is typically developed from clues found in the available documentation or a tip from a party with insider knowledge. It is possible for an attorney to send subpoenas to random banks, hoping to come across bank accounts related to an investigation. In reality, however, that is not very practical, so this strategy is not often used.

Bank documentation can be time consuming to analyze. Multiple transfers between bank accounts can also muddy the waters when investigators are attempting to trace the flow of money. It is not uncommon for people engaged in fraud schemes to make multiple transfers of funds between several accounts in order to conceal the true source or use of funds. Despite the challenges, bank documents are so useful because they provide proof of who or what company paid or received money. That proof might include forged signatures or endorsements, or names of fake companies or people. Even still, a check like that will contain other clues that may help unravel things.

In late 2004, the Check 21 law took effect in the United States. This law made it possible for banks to transfer money to and from one another without presenting a physical check. Instead, banks can electronically transmit an image of the original check (referred to as a "substitute check"). This law makes the image the legal equivalent of the actual check, even in court proceedings. Initially, some people thought that this law would make it more difficult for fraud investigators to do their jobs. Many banks take images of the checks and destroy the actual checks. Aren't those checks integral to the fraud investigation? No. So long as an image of the check exists, the fraud investigator's work can still be done.

The widespread use of images over paper checks, however, has made things a little less convenient for some fraud investigators. A bank statement with actual canceled checks is easy to examine, as the investigator can quickly page through a stack of checks and examine the backs of checks as necessary. A bank statement with digital images may not be so easy to examine. Some banks do not automatically include images of the backs of checks, which are a critical component to fraud investigations. In this case, those images may need to be requested from the bank.

While there may be some small inconveniences as a result of not having the actual checks, those have been outweighed by availability of documentation from the banks. Companies no longer have to wait for bank employees to research checks by hand and look for microfiche copies of the checks, a process that was expensive and time consuming. The increased use of technology means many banks are able to produce account documentation with a few clicks of a computer mouse. That convenience is invaluable, and there is a higher level of accuracy, because the investigator is not relying on a human to identify the checks in question.

Bank documentation can also include paperwork related to loans and mortgages. The items could include valuable information about a person's or company's financial situation, give clues about accounts at other financial institutions, and help uncover inconsistencies in representations made by the party in question. Loan documents usually require listings of assets and liabilities, with some detail required. This information should be compared to financial statements or other documentation related to assets and liabilities.

Do the numbers agree reasonably? If they do not, should this be investigated further? Do there appear to be assets or liabilities that have not been disclosed previously? Does this nondisclosure have any implications for the case? Does it appear that there has been an attempt to hide any of this information?

This documentation can be invaluable in identifying real estate, bank accounts, and investment accounts that might otherwise have gone undiscovered. People or companies applying for loans usually want to make their applications look as favorable as possible, and are likely to include all assets on them. That provides a clear benefit to a fraud investigator, who often encounters people and companies that want to hide as many assets as possible.

Investment Accounts

Records of investment account activity can serve many of the same purposes that bank account records serve. Again, the problem exists with individuals and companies having multiple accounts, potentially with different brokers. The fraud investigator is going to rely on clues developed when analyzing available documentation to find evidence of other accounts.

Like a bank, an investment company can provide detailed account records that will support the flow of funds in and out of the accounts. Inexperienced fraudsters are not always as careful about their use of investment accounts as they might be about bank accounts. They simply do not realize sometimes that their investment account records can be accessed in the same way bank records can.

Tax Documentation

Tax records can be useful in a variety of different ways, depending on the type of case you are working. In a case that involves verifying sales or expenses for a company, the business income tax returns can help you do so. Sometimes discrepancies are noted between financial statements and tax returns, which can be troubling. Fraud investigators often consider the tax returns to be the "official" numbers, as those were signed and sent to the government as true and correct.

In cases involving the earnings of individuals, such as disability insurance fraud, the personal income tax returns will help verify earnings from year to year. They also help identify sources of income, which could be important information for the investigation as a whole. There may be clues about other investments or business ownership by the target. Tax returns could also give an indication of the financial condition of a person, potentially indicating a motive for fraud.

Sales tax records can be used to help verify monthly, quarterly, or annual sales in a case in which sales levels are in question. A fraud investigator may want to confirm a downturn in sales during a particular period of time, or may be looking for information about sales trends throughout the years. Sales tax records are very helpful in this regard, especially if they are available on a monthly basis.

The distinct advantage of tax records is the ability to receive verification of the records from the taxing authorities. The subject of an investigation may be responsible for producing tax returns to the investigator. How will the forensic accountant or fraud investigator know whether those are authentic? They can verify the information on the returns by contacting the tax agency directly and requesting verification, either with the taxpayer's consent or a court order.

Credit Reports

Consent is needed to obtain an individual's credit report, but if an investigator is able to get it, a lot of useful information can be found within the credit report. It will show current and previous employers, addresses, and credit accounts. It will give clues to the financial condition of the person and will also identify related parties, such as a spouse or other person holding a joint credit account. Real estate mortgages and auto loans will be listed, providing clues about assets owned. Details about credit cards held and balances over time will be part of the report. Bankruptcies, tax liens, and judgments will also be a part of a credit report.

The reliability of credit reports is notoriously questionable, as the credit reporting agencies are known for having a high instance of inaccuracy in their records. Information found via a credit report should be verified, if possible, from a secondary source of information. Ideally, the fraud investigator should go directly to the creditor or another source of records to verify any information on which the investigator will substantially rely. The information on a credit report should not be considered authoritative. Rather, it should be considered a good starting point for finding information about a person.

Medical Records

In cases involving individuals and injury or illness, medical records may be needed to support contentions about injuries or disability. Disability insurance claims, personal injury lawsuits, and workers' compensation cases might all require the medical records of a person. Typically, the insurance companies and attorneys have procedures in place to get medical records, and the expert can access them if necessary.

In a financial fraud case, the details of the medical records are often not relevant to the fraud investigator. The ultimate medical condition of the subject of the investigation will usually be determined by an expert in the medical field, and the fraud investigator will rely on that opinion in conducting her or his work.

Sometimes the medical status is essentially irrelevant to the fraud investigator. Often, a forensic accountant or fraud investigator is simply asked to analyze the financial details of a situation. For example, the investigator may be asked to render an opinion on whether a person's income increased or decreased over a particular period of time. The fact that a decline in income may result from a medical situation is not a concern in this type of case. The question to be answered is only whether the person's income increased or decreased.

It is important to find out what type of consideration the client wants the fraud investigator to give the medical records. Unless a fraud investigator has medical expertise, the use of the medical records in formulating an opinion on the numbers should likely be limited.

Specialized Records

Depending on the type of case the fraud investigator is working, specialized records should be obtained. For example, a personal injury case may include a report by a vocational expert, giving an opinion about future job opportunities for the injured person. A case of suspected arson on a business property might include a report by an arson expert. A breakup of business partners might include a valuation report completed by an independent expert.

It is important to think creatively and ask a lot of questions to determine whether there are any relevant pieces of information like this available for inspection by the investigator. It is not the client's job to know what the fraud investigator needs to do her or his job. It is the investigator's responsibility to proactively seek out relevant information, resources, and reports to support her or his conclusions.

Public Records

Many public records sources can be invaluable in a fraud investigation. At first glance, some of them may not seem all that important, but the investigator must recognize that small nuggets of information can be pulled from a variety of sources and assembled in a way that significantly benefits a case. It has never been easier for a fraud investigator to tap into the wealth of knowledge contained in public records, especially as more of them become available online. They can be used to locate people and property, value property, research the backgrounds of individuals and companies, and verify information found from other sources.

Some government records, like income tax records, are private. Others, like marriage records, real estate transfers, and business filings, are public. It is important to be able to differentiate between public and private records so that the investigator can actively seek out the records that are legally publicly available.

Court Records

Civil and criminal court records are widely available on a local, state, and federal level. More information is becoming accessible online, but most jurisdictions limit their online information to general case information, including parties, attorneys, dates of hearings and motions, and results of the cases. To get the actual filings and documents, unsealed court records must often be requested in person at courthouses across the country. The federal court system does offer copies of filings online, accessed through PACER (Public Access to Electronic Court Records) for a minimal per-page charge.

It is always a good idea to contact the clerk of courts to see whether records can be obtained without having to go to the courthouse, especially if it is in another city or state. Sometimes the clerk can send, fax, or e-mail documents if proper payment arrangements are made and the local rules allow for it. In areas in which records can be provided only in-person, consider contacting a company that contracts out those services so you are not forced to go there yourself.

Civil court records can help establish relationships between people and companies, and can provide information on business operations and financial conditions of individuals and companies. They might provide clues to a person's financial situation and potential troubles, such as divorces, child support, judgments, repossessions, or foreclosures. These kinds of cases can contain a wealth of personal and financial information that might help shed light on your investigation. A history of lawsuits could indicate something about a person's past business and personal relationships and patterns that may be material to an investigation.

It is important to search more than just an individual's name or a company's name when researching civil court records. Search for records for related parties (relatives, friends, co-workers, known business associates) to see whether there is anything found pertinent to your investigation. The most relevant information will likely be found in court records tied directly to the person under investigation, but it never hurts to check related parties.

Probate court records detail the happenings after a person dies and assets are being divided, sometimes with a will and sometimes without a will. The records that will be most useful in a fraud investigation concern the distribution of assets, providing not only information about potential financial issues, but also potential motives behind disputes between people. These records may also contain information about relationships between people and business entities.

Criminal court records are important to show the criminal history of an individual. Offenses can range from traffic tickets and ordinance violations to misdemeanors and felonies. It is not a good idea to draw too many conclusions from the type of charge or even what the charge was called. Details of situations and people involved can play a big part in how an offense is charged and whether a plea is offered. It is important to look at actual court documents to determine the details of the situation if the information from the criminal records is going to play a part in your investigation and conclusions.

Imagine how embarrassing it could be to draw a conclusion based on what the charge was called, only to find out that the situation giving rise to the charges was quite different from what you assumed. As an example, there are many situations in which a defendant pleads guilty to disorderly conduct. This ordinance violation or criminal charge is often used by law enforcement as a catch-all when other more specific laws do not address a situation or there are other circumstances that warrant it. A fraud investigator can't assume that the situation involved a brawl or other physical altercation, when the fact remains that the situation could be anything from a traffic accident to threatening phone calls. Police reports and court records are critical in determining what actually happened in a situation.

Bankruptcy court records will show all the creditors of an individual or business and the amounts owed to them. Assets owned at the time of the bankruptcy filing will also be listed, and sometimes substantial detail is included. These records aid in analyzing the financial status of a person or company, and may also give clues to relationships between businesses and people.

Other relevant court records that are increasingly more widely available on the Internet include tax court, naturalization court, and a variety of hearing boards. When looking for unusual types of court records, do not give up easily. There are so many court records available online, although sometimes they are not easy to find. Search high and low before giving up. When searching online court records, be sure that you are aware of what is and is not included in the database you are using. Sometimes a particular type of case might be excluded from the online records, and you may need to know that. There may also be a particular jurisdiction not included in the records, or cases prior to a particular date may not be available.

Also be careful when relying on court records gathered online. Many websites have disclaimers about accuracy. Depending on how you intend to use the records you find, it might be worthwhile to request copies of the actual records from the court in order to verify what you have found online. Do not assume just because a search has not turned up any records that there are not any records for the person or business in question. Consider the effect of misspellings or name changes, as well as the possibility that errors in record keeping might prevent you from finding certain records.

Arrest Records

The information provided in arrest records can be valuable, because it can point to problems a person is having. It may also give information about addresses, family, associates, vehicles, or other people, places, and things involved in a situation. Arrest records are freely available in person at police stations, but their availability online is very limited. Many local newspapers publish arrest records, so that can be a secondary source either in print or online.

It is important to note that law enforcement records like police reports can contain errors and inaccuracies. A police report is an opportunity for a police officer to document what she or he saw, as well as what witnesses to a situation saw. That does not mean that the facts will all be included in the report, or that everything in the report will be accurate. Use the information in police reports and arrest records carefully, and when possible, use court records to shed further light on the facts of a situation.

Incarceration Records

State inmate records are available online in some states. For other states, the records may be available through other means. The Federal Bureau of Prisons has a searchable database that gives the status of past and present inmates and their location, if still incarcerated. Incarceration records can confirm the whereabouts of people during certain time periods. It may also be necessary to verify their release from prison, as compared to the sentence received in a case.

Sex Offender Databases

Most states have at least some sex offender database information online. These records can help confirm addresses, convictions, and incarceration histories. Because of the sensitive nature of these situations, it is advisable to verify details of convictions with actual court records if the information is going to be relied on in a fraud investigation.

Vital Records

Included in vital records are birth certificates, death certificates, marriage certificates, and divorce records. Not all states allow these records to be completely public, so some access is restricted. If an investigator can get access to them, she or he can find a wealth of information inside.

Birth records can provide information about parents, their addresses, their employment, the place of birth, and the delivering doctor. Death certificates contain the cause of death, place of death, and next of kin, and can point an investigator to probate filings, which may have a lot of financial and other information in them. Death can be confirmed via the Social Security Death Index, which includes the name, date of birth, place of issuance of Social Security Number, date of death, and last residence.

Marriage records offer a bride's maiden name, addresses of both spouses, and information on witnesses. Divorce records may be maintained with vital records, or may be kept with civil court records. In either case, they provide much information about the parties, children, jobs, assets, liabilities, and possibly detailed histories about all of these.

Voter Records

Voter registration records can help you find someone, as voting records are almost always public. States each have an agency that oversees voting, and most also have a central point for voter data. Accessibility of the records varies by state, but it is important to know that it is possible to get the records in many places.

Corporate Records

States track registrations of corporations, partnerships, and limited liability companies (LLCs), usually in the Secretary of State's office. Most states collect registration information, including the name of the business, the registered agent, and the address. Most states do not keep track of details like owners or board of directors members, although a few may gather this information and make it available either on paper or over the Internet.

Businesses that are not organized as corporations, partnerships, or LLCs may still need to register with a state or local government so that there is a record of the business and its owners. These records can be referred to as "doing business as" (DBA), assumed names, or fictitious names filings.

Like other public records, the amount of information available online about businesses is increasing, and many states make their databases searchable by the general public.

Real Estate Records

Property ownership and tax records can provide a wealth of information about people, assets, and relationships. The records are typically divided into two groups: property ownership records found at the recorder's office (also called register of deeds) and property tax records found at the assessor's office. Information contained in these records will include ownership (past and present), sales price, legal description, buildings on the property, value of the property, tax bills, and tax payment information. There will also be information on mortgages on properties, as the holder of a mortgage must file legal documents to protect its interest in the property for which the mortgage is given.

There are lots of real estate records to be found online, but they are not always the easiest to search. Often, you are not able to search by the name of the owner. Rather, you can search only for a particular piece of property and find the details on that parcel. It certainly does not make things easy when an investigator is trying to find hidden property.

Uniform Commercial Code (UCC) Filings

UCC filings are recorded when businesses receive financing that is secured by assets such as equipment, inventory, accounts receivable, furniture, or fixtures. A mortgage is filed for financing related to real estate, and a UCC filing is for financing linked to personal property. UCC filings are publicly available and are important to determine a company's lenders and who has rights to the company's assets. These filings are recorded at a county or state level (or possibly both), depending on the state in which the filing occurred. UCC records are widely available online.

Tax Liens

Although tax records are generally of a private nature, unpaid state and federal taxes can become public. More states have been publishing databases of tax "deadbeats," often citing the individuals and businesses who owe the most in overdue taxes.

Liens against personal property or real estate for unpaid taxes are public filings, and a lien can be filed for unpaid sales, income, withholding, unemployment, or personal property taxes. When a tax lien is placed on property, the owner generally is not legally able to sell or refinance the property without first satisfying the lien. Tax liens provide valuable information about the financial health of a business or individual. Clearly, significant unpaid taxes are a sign of financial troubles.

The severity of the troubles may also be judged by the type of taxes that are unpaid. Sales taxes and withholding taxes represent money collected from others on behalf of the government, and are required to be remitted fairly quickly. Nonpayment of those taxes sometimes signals the most serious financial troubles because they are pursued very aggressively by the government and carry with them significant penalties and interest when unpaid.

Driver and Motor Vehicle Records

The availability of driver and motor vehicle records varies by state. Some limit what can be accessed and who accesses it, and the keepers of the records are becoming more selective about access. If an investigator is able to access driver records, she or he will get information like name, address, date of birth, driving history, license type, and restrictions. Motor vehicle records will include name, address, vehicle identification number, and titleholder.

Academic Records

Colleges and universities regularly verify information about degrees earned, both over the telephone and in writing. Typically, definitive proof of a degree must be requested in writing.

Alumni directories or websites can provide more information about an individual, including an address and employer. Some sites even allow alumni to provide additional biographical data that can be informative to the investigator. You may be surprised to see how much information people are willing to provide to their alumni association, because they want their schoolmates to be aware of their life changes and career accomplishments.

Professional Licensing

States require licensing for all kinds of professionals, including doctors, hairstylists, private detectives, physical therapists, accountants, lawyers, and many more. From these records, you can find information about a person's credentials and certifications, as well as possibly their employers, address, and disciplinary history.

Stock Ownership

The SEC maintains buy and sell information for stockholders with more than a 10% interest in public companies. Stock ownership records are also maintained for officers and directors of public companies. These records are maintained in searchable databases, which might help the investigator find out about significant ownership interests in any public company. This is another tool used to link individuals and businesses to one another.

Intellectual Property

The U.S. Patent and Trademark Office maintains a wealth of information on copyrights, patents, and trademarks for which companies apply. This information can give clues about a business and its operations, and may also hint to some sort of value that the company has by way of intellectual property.

Business and Industry Databases

Companies like Hoovers and Dun & Bradstreet have made a business out of selling information about companies and the industries in which they operate. Websites like theirs will often offer "teaser" information about companies in an attempt to get a consumer to buy a full report on a company.

The databases can contain information about a company, its owners and officers, compensation of executives, financial statements, key ratios and metrics, and creditors. Do not avoid these resources just because of the cost involved in getting the records. The amount of information they have about companies is sometimes astounding, and even if there is a fee involved in accessing the information, it is often well worth the money. It would take an investigator hours to pull together what one simple search and a reasonable fee on a site like this provides.

The Internet and Search Engines

The proliferation of online databases and the Internet in general has had a major impact on the fraud investigator's work. A person no longer needs to physically go to a courthouse to get most records, as many jurisdictions offer lots of information about cases online. Free tools like simple search engines have made it infinitely easier to find information on people and companies. Information that was likely thought of as obscure and difficult to find a couple of decades ago is now right at the fraud investigator's fingertips.

For example, it is now easy to search thousands of newspapers at once. Who would have thought that simple research like this might give away the whereabouts of a fraudster on a particular date, link a suspected fraudster with a politician, or document a thief's participation in an event?

Social networking sites add to the volume of information available on the Internet. Users have been known to create detailed profiles, which include information on friends, vital statistics, work and education history, and many personal details. It is possible to see whom these people have "connected" with on the various sites, which might provide the investigator with valuable information about business and personal relationships.

While the ability to find all kinds of information on the Internet has helped fraud investigators, the ease of finding this information has in some ways given clients greater expectations. The client knows what is available on the Internet for the person who knows where to look, so they are expecting more than ever from fraud investigators.

The increased availability of information has also placed an additional burden on the fraud investigator: determining the accuracy and validity of the information. It is important to determine whether information is coming from legitimate, reliable sources. There are many sources of bogus information on the Internet, and these sites often masquerade as legitimate, reliable sources of information. There is so much propaganda on the Internet, that it can sometimes be difficult to sort through the information to determine what is legitimate. The job of verifying information and sources of information should not be taken lightly. The credibility of an investigator is on the line each time she or he relies on a source.

Making the best use of records available on the Internet means being aggressive in searching and seeking out information. Effectively using search engines is an art unto itself, and a fraud investigator should work on learning this art in order to find better, more useful search results.

Searches should not be limited to a person or company in question. Search relatives, friends, neighbors, co-workers, and business associates who might provide clues about a suspect or witness. Use alternative spellings of names in the case that information was recorded with a misspelling. Be sure to find out whether a suspect has a maiden name or has otherwise changed her or his name legally or informally. Determine whether the person has a nickname or abbreviated name that should be searched. Look for variations in company names, from changes in spellings, to use of acronyms, to changes in legal name. Seek out information on the names of divisions or operating entities related to the company. Inquire about spin-off companies, separate companies that exist only to service the company in question, and special-purpose entities that might be important.

An Internet search for information on a business or person should go beyond conventional search engines, too. Even the most comprehensive search engines have indexed only a small fraction of the websites available on the World Wide Web. Competent fraud investigators will utilize lesser-known resources to expand their searches for relevant data and evidence.

CHAPTER 6

Investigative Techniques

The examination of physical evidence, such as documents, is often the heart of a fraud investigation. Paper records, such as bank statements, canceled checks, written contracts, and real estate closing documents, are typical examples of documents that will be integral to a fraud investigation.

We have already discussed the proper way to handle and preserve evidence (Chapter 3). The fraud investigator may also need to have the documents authenticated, and experts in forged and counterfeit documents can help. Handwriting experts can confirm the authenticity of signatures and determine whether writing has been altered. With the help of technology, the origins of ink can be discovered, the type of copy machine can be determined, and alterations or concealments on a page can be revealed.

If the documents are accepted as authentic (or true and correct copies of the originals), then the investigator jumps into examining them, extracting the information necessary to do the investigation. The investigation is less about the pieces of paper themselves, and more about the information those pieces of paper provide.

The proliferation of digital data and documents means that most investigations will go far beyond pieces of paper. Fraud investigators must be proficient with computerized records as well, and must be able to work with them as skillfully as they might work with paper evidence.

In this chapter, we will talk about some of the most basic techniques for gathering and analyzing information in a fraud investigation. The subsequent four chapters will focus more on specific areas of concern in a fraud investigation, red flags that might tip off the investigator to a problem, and techniques used to examine these things.

Corporate Background Checks

Verifying details about a company can go far beyond simply checking the Secretary of State's office for registration information. As we saw in Chapter 5, a lot of information is available via public records and the Internet. Fraud investigators need to be creative in looking for sources of information about companies. There is an ever-expanding pool of information available on the Internet, but it needs to be accessed and used responsibly by verifying the accuracy and reliability of the sources and the information.

Public companies usually have more information publicly available, as the Securities and Exchange Commission (SEC) requires them to disclose information about the company, its operations, locations, board of directors, financial statements, and financing agreements. Private companies do not have nearly as much information available about them, which is one advantage of being privately held. That does not mean, however, that private companies cannot be thoroughly investigated. They can, even when limited information is made available by the company. Many resources can help piece together information about the company's operations, ownership, management, and financial strength.

Individual Background Checks

Any seasoned investigator will tell you that the best background checks are the ones done *before* a person is hired. It is often difficult to get real information about applicants from previous employers because of the potential for litigation. Even in states in which the laws protect a former employer who provides truthful information about someone, many companies still fear litigation and are reluctant to provide negative information about an applicant.

But whether or not a background check was done prior to hiring an employee, a background check can still be a good investigative tool. They are best performed by licensed private investigators who specialize in background checks on individuals. They have the most experience and typically the best access to important databases and other sources of information.

A simple background check is easy for most fraud investigators and forensic accountants to do. Just running a person's name through a standard database that details previous addresses, properties owned, spouses, and the like isn't hard to do. When you need a deeper background check that involves verifying credentials, examining prior business interests, searching for court records, and the like, that is when the professional background checkers should be called in.

Searching for Friends, Family, and Associates

One key in fraud investigations can be the identification of parties related to the person being investigated. Relationships such as these that are kept secret are often undisclosed for special reasons. Take, for example, a business owner who is making a claim for disability insurance benefits. The insurance company looks for evidence that the claimant is actually disabled, which will include both the medical cause as well as the inability to perform job functions and earn a living.

Suppose that the business owner represents that since he will never be able to work again, he has sold his business to someone, which is proof that he will have no earnings. Under normal circumstances, this might be completely legitimate. But what if it was later determined that the business was actually sold to his brother-in-law? This small fact was never disclosed by the claimant, even when asked about related-party transactions. The concealment of the family relationship might be an indicator that the sale of the business was not legitimately an arm's-length transaction. It is possible that the original owner sold to a related party in order to protect his interest and to secretly continue to work and earn income, even after representing to the insurance company that he could not work again.

The situation could potentially be completely legitimate, and the sale might truly be a full disposition of the claimant's interest in the company. Yet the fact that the family relationship was concealed will certainly raise questions. If there was nothing to hide, why wouldn't the claimant disclose the family ties?

There are many other ways that associates of someone under investigation can provide investigative leads. Consider an investigation of a shell company scheme, in which it is found that the suspect's next-door neighbor is the registered agent of the shell company. That information could be a vital tidbit that could go a long way toward proving the fraud.

What about concealed relationships between employees at a company? There can be fraud risks when spouses, siblings, love interests, or friends are employed at a company. The potential for collusion is always there, so these relationships should be eyed closely. They should be examined even more carefully if the relationships were concealed, especially if the company has a policy requiring disclosure of such situations.

Surveillance

Depending on the type of case being investigated, surveillance of people can be a particularly effective way of gathering information. Many states require those who are engaging in surveillance to be licensed private investigators, so it is important to make sure that you are following the laws before you start watching people.

Surveillance in general means observing people, places, and movements. It is common to videotape almost all surveillance these days, but that is optional. An investigator could engage in surveillance and just take notes or rely on her or his memory of the events. Videotaped evidence is more difficult to refute, which is why it is so common to capture these things on video.

Stationary video cameras in the workplace are a common form of surveillance, but employers have to be careful to also follow state laws when monitoring employees. Monitoring e-mail, instant messages, and other computer activities can be done legally as well, but a knowledgeable attorney should be involved to help ensure compliance with laws.

Digital Data Analysis

While the average consumer may think that the Information Age and the existence of the Internet have made getting away with fraud easier, that may not necessarily be the case. In some ways, it may be easier to initiate a fraud. For example, it previously required someone's signature on a check to get money out of a bank account. Now, the proliferation of electronic transfers may make it easier to get money out of the bank account, especially if there is a lack of internal controls in a company.

Technology has changed the way fraud is committed, but it has also created paper trails that often make it easier to detect and investigate a fraud. Every digital transaction leaves behind a trail of digital evidence, which a fraudster may not necessarily be able to dissociate herself or himself from. Commercially available software has made it possible for companies to analyze a huge amount of data in a very short period of time, increasing the chances that unusual activity will be detected quickly.

Software can offer companies two key advantages in monitoring their systems and detecting fraud. One option is performing tests at various intervals on data sets from the company's accounting system to detect anomalies or indicators of fraud. The software is designed to detect some of the most common signs of errors and irregularities, and companies can use the software on some or all of their transactions on a planned or surprise basis. The second option is to use software to continuously monitor a company's accounting systems. The software can help management detect control problems as they are occurring, and also help potential frauds to be identified almost in real time.

Some of the things that software might identify as problems include:

- Unusually high number of transactions just below a certain level of authority for a supervisor
- High number of manual disbursements
- Frequently occurring transactions in large, round-dollar amounts
- Unusual patterns for write-offs or adjustments
- Evidence of payment of duplicate invoices
- Recurring instances of partial payments by customers
- Identification of suspicious addresses when comparing data on employees, customers, and vendors
- Vendor billings in excess of budgeted amounts due to improper coding of payments
- Vendor price increases at a rate exceeding the rates of similar vendors
- Changing purchasing patterns that suggest favoring a particular vendor, which may not be in line with management's approved purchasing plan

The real advantage to data analysis with computer software is the ability to examine large data sets in a short period of time. Depending on the software used, there will be limitations, so analyzing the data digitally will not be foolproof. There can be cases in which a fraudulent payment to a vendor does not have any red flags that cause the software to identify it as irregular. There can also be problems with flagged items, in which tens of thousands of records are identified as irregular based on the software's criteria, and someone has to manually examine each one.

It should also be clear that analysis of data using commercial software is not the only piece of a fraud investigation. Once the software identifies potential problems, the fraud investigator must fully investigate each issue to determine whether there is evidence of fraud, or whether the items identified are explained and supported by legitimate documentation. Digital data analysis is a tool used to enhance fraud investigations, but not a substitute for good investigative work.

Computer Forensics

As mentioned in Chapter 3, a computer forensics expert can be of great assistance during a fraud investigation. It is not uncommon for an employee who commits fraud to attempt to destroy or cover up computerized data. Sometimes their methods are very crude and amount to nothing more than hitting the delete key, without realizing that the document is not really deleted. Other methods are more thought-out and effective. A fraudster might install software designed to "wipe" a computer hard drive of data, corrupt critical databases, or sabotage certain files if someone tries to access them. Those methods are often more effective, but some can still be thwarted by a competent computer forensics person, who may be able to salvage some useful data from the computer.

A computer forensics expert is typically well-versed in securing digital evidence to preserve it for future courtroom activity, as well as recovering data that may have been accidentally or purposely deleted or destroyed. Even when someone intends to delete files from a computer, pieces of evidence may remain on that computer for a long time. Harvesting these bits of data may be critical to a fraud investigation.

Interviewing Witnesses and Suspects

Any book on fraud investigations would not be complete if it did not discuss the issue of conducting interviews in the course of an investigation. Volumes have been written on this topic, and investigators can even seek out certifications in interviewing techniques. This section of the book is intended to be merely a brief look at interviewing. It will cover some of the high points of interviewing, but not the details of the techniques that may be used to elicit admissions from suspects.

Fraud investigators are continually in question-and-answer mode when trying to understand a company, its operations, the players, and the suspected fraud. Much of this is done informally, with an information exchange between employees and investigators. A big part of interviewing involves having the right demeanor and body language. People who are uninvolved in the fraud and are giving you information want to feel comfortable doing so, and they want to know that the investigator is listening. That has to be accomplished while directing the discussions so that time is not wasted on much unnecessary commentary. There must be a focus on the items that will help solve the case.

The best interviewers are able to connect with those being interviewed in a way that makes them want to help and provide information. They have a way of guiding the discussion while listening to the person giving information. They do not interrupt a lot, and even when they need to focus the interviewee, they do it in a way that does not seem like an interruption. Excellent interviewers have the ability to put the interviewee at ease. They are professional in their demeanor, yet relaxed enough that the interviewee feels comfortable sharing information.

Before going into a high-stakes interview, the fraud investigator must plan the interview. Putting together an outline will help meet the objectives and ensure that important information and questions are not missed. The closer the interviewee is to the fraud, the more helpful it is to have lots of information about the situation gathered before the interview. So, for instance, if you are interviewing the main suspect, you want to have the bulk of the investigation done so that you go in knowing solid facts. It will be much harder for the suspect to fool you if you have done this, because you already know a lot about the fraud based on your work.

Do not try to pretend you are part of a television drama in which you walk into the interview with little knowledge or evidence and trick the suspect into a full confession. That does not usually happen in the real world, which is why it is better to be armed with lots of facts before conducting a critical interview.

If you are interviewing a potential accomplice or someone close to the suspect because of her or his position in the company (e.g., the suspect's personal assistant), you should have plenty of information already uncovered. But you do not necessarily have to be done (or almost done) with the fraud investigation. You will be looking to this person to provide some background information to help you with your investigation, so it makes sense that you still have work to do when you go into this interview.

The room in which the interview takes place should be private and free from distractions. You do not want other employees looking in windows or otherwise interrupting the interview. You do not want a ringing phone to interrupt a critical line of questioning.

A few tips for questioning an employee:

- Interview only one person at a time. You do not want the answers of one person to influence the responses of the other.
- Be cautious with note-taking activities. Some notes usually need to be taken, especially on very technical issues. However, taking notes can be a turn-off to the respondent, so the interviewer should limit note-taking as much as possible.
- Use short, easy-to-understand questions. Avoid complex or compound questions.
- Try to avoid a lot of "yes" and "no" questions. Open-ended questions will help you gather more information.
- Allow the interviewee ample time to answer the question and ask her or him to expound on incomplete answers.
- Encourage interviewees to provide a factual basis for their answers. For example, you might ask, "Why do you think that's what happened?" or "What did you see that led you to that conclusion?" or "How do you know that he was the one who took the blank checks?"
- Keep the interview on track and do not let the interviewee talk at length about unrelated things. (Some do this to be evasive, while others do this because they are nervous, and still others do it because it is just their nature to ramble aimlessly.)
- Do not reveal too much evidence during the interview. You are there to gather information, not provide a lot of information.
- Maintain control of the interview. You are in charge.

An interview can be divided into five parts: (1) introduction, (2) information gathering, (3) assessment, (4) admission seeking, and (5) closing. During the *introduction*, the interviewer tells the respondent about the purpose of the interview and gets her or him to agree to cooperate. Put the person at ease and establish a rapport, which will help you gather as much information as possible.

Avoid menacing titles like "fraud investigator" and simply say that you are working to gather some information for an assignment. Remember that your body language will help set the tone for the interview, so give the interviewee plenty of space, maintain open body positions to indicate you are approachable, and use gestures (such as nodding and leaning forward) that make it clear you are interested in what the respondent has to say.

The *information-gathering* portion of the interview is focused on gathering facts from the respondent. The fraud investigator might need information about the accounting process, certain documents, employee responsibilities, or specific workplace situations.

Questions asked could be:

- *Closed*. Questions of a closed nature require only a yes or no answer. Examples: Are you responsible for making the bank deposits? Did you work last week Monday? Do you understand the expense reporting policies of this company?
- *Open*. These questions require a narrative response from the respondent. It is preferable to use open questions, because they help gather the most information and create an atmosphere that is conducive to conversation. Examples: Could you explain the system for receiving and recording customer payments on their accounts? Tell me why you didn't go straight to the bank on Friday when you left here with the bank deposit? Can you explain how an employee's expense report is processed and approved?
- *Leading*. In a leading question, the interviewer essentially provides the answer within the question. Examples: So you were on vacation that week and did not see what happened to the records storage room? Is it correct that after punching in yesterday, you went directly to Bill's office to get instructions from him on a new project?

One good way to work through the information and questions is to go from the general to the more specific. Start with questions aimed at gathering general information about a department, the employees, and the operations. Then, when a foundation has been established, begin to ask more specific questions about who is involved with certain things or what happened on certain days.

It is also helpful to begin the interview with questions that do not cause a respondent to become defensive, hostile, or suspicious. The goal of the interviewer is to put the respondent at ease to facilitate getting as much information as possible. Even when interviewing the prime suspect in the fraud, it is still appropriate to put her or him at ease to create an atmosphere that encourages information exchange.

During the interview, you may utilize *assessment* questions to help determine the respondent's credibility. Many clues about deception can come out during this line of questioning. The interviewer will want to be familiar with the speech patterns, body language, and method of answering questions. Courses or books on interviewing cover this information at great length, and should be consulted by the fraud investigator who wants to advance her or his level of interviewing skill.

Admission-seeking questions are part of advanced interviewing skills. When you are reasonably certain of a respondent's involvement in a fraud, you may use these questions to either clear an innocent person or get a guilty person to confess. When trying to get a guilty party to confess, it should be clear that the interviewer already knows she or he has committed the fraud. If the respondent thinks you are unsure, the probability of a confession goes down significantly.

The interviewer might accuse the suspect of committing the fraud and observe the reaction. Questions will arise like, "Why did you do this?" The suspect may deny the fraud, but the interviewer should interrupt the denials. The interviewer might move to reasoning with the suspect, possibly showing some key pieces of evidence to prove that the suspect is guilty. Only a limited amount of evidence should be shared.

Even though you may know that the person is guilty, do not expect her or him to confess if you are intent on conveying that people who commit fraud are bad. The admission will be much easier to get if you help the respondent rationalize the behavior. Rationalization allows the fraudster to not be a "bad person." The suspect instead is portrayed during the interview as someone who had a logical reason for his or her behavior.

The interviewer can offer the rationalization to the suspect, helping to make the fraud acceptable in the respondent's mind, and make it easier for the person to admit committing the fraud. Examples of common rationalizations include financial problems, unfair treatment, inadequate pay, family problems, on-the-job stress, revenge, a minor moral infraction, and a genuine need.

In *closing* the interview, you should confirm the information you have gathered and clarify any issues that may be confusing. The interviewer may also try to confirm a motive for the fraud, determine who else was involved, and attempt to secure evidence. For example, you may try to get the suspect to sign a release authorizing you to access her or his bank records. Ask the interviewee whether there is any other important information that she or he would like to share, and whether there is anyone else you should talk to. Ask whether it is okay to talk again if you need more information.

A few final tips for effective interviewing:

- *Do not promise confidentiality.* You cannot be sure in which direction the investigation will go, and the respondent's information could be integral to future work. You cannot be sure what the client will ultimately do with the information gathered during the investigation, so it would be unfair to promise confidentiality.
- *Do not negotiate with the interviewee.* You are not in a position to promise anything in exchange for information.
- *Do not attempt to hold the respondent against her or his will.* If the interviewee wants to leave the interview, you can briefly try to talk her or him out of it, but do not try to detain the person.

Confirmation with Customers and Vendors

Confirming account balances is a typical technique used during traditional financial statement audits. A similar technique can be used in fraud investigations to confirm activity with customers and vendors. This is particularly useful when an employee is suspected of altering records, stealing payments, or otherwise attempting to hide a theft.

If a customer or vendor is in collusion with an employee inside the client's company, the confirmation of account activity and balances might not be terribly useful. But unless some evidence indicates collusion, this simple investigative method can yield very useful information.

Data and documents coming from a third party can often be more reliable than internal documents to which a suspect had access. Those third-party documents are less likely to be altered or destroyed, making them a key piece of an investigation.

In coming chapters, we will discuss specific red flags and analytical procedures that may help an investigator detect suspicious customer or vendor accounts. The process of confirming account activity will help verify whether fraud may have occurred with these accounts. For example, suppose an employee purposely causes a vendor account to be paid $75,000, when the vendor has actually submitted an invoice for $60,000 to the company. The employee then asks the vendor to send the excess funds back to his attention. When the check for $15,000 arrives, the rogue employee steals it and cashes it for himself. He may have adjusted the company's records so that the original overpayment appears instead to be a legitimate payment to the vendor.

If the fraud investigator attempts to confirm account activity with the vendor, there is a pretty good chance that this fraud can come to light. The vendor responds to the confirmation request with a printout of the account activity for the year. The fraud investigator compares the company's records (which show a payment of $75,000) to the vendor's records (which show an invoice of $60,000, a payment received of $75,000, and a refund of $15,000). The fraud investigator now has evidence suggesting a fraud has occurred. Without the vendor confirmation, this information likely would not have come to light unless someone else looked at the expense account and suspected the numbers were too high. Even then, there might not be any evidence to support that suspicion, and the fraud could easily go undetected.

Confirmation is an old-fashioned method of investigating fraud, yet its benefits are undeniable. It is easy to do and comes at a relatively low cost. It brings in third-party information, which has a greater level of reliability, assuming the third parties are not involved in a fraud scheme with the company's employees. No special skills are required to carry out the confirmation, and analysis of the results can be done by less experienced fraud investigators.

Creativity and the Fraud Investigator

You probably do not normally think of fraud investigators as being creative, but that is simply not the case. The best investigators are creative. Looking for ways to verify data or find clues about fraud involves thinking outside the normal parameters of business to come up with sources and ideas.

Occasionally a reformed criminal with the uncanny ability to put himself in the shoes of the suspect can make an excellent fraud investigator. He may ask himself, "How would I commit fraud in this company?" One such fraud investigator is Barry Minkow of ZZZZ Best Carpet Cleaning. He was one of the youngest people ever to take a company public in the United States, and ended up being a very young federal prison inmate because of the massive fraud he perpetrated via ZZZZ Best.

Several years after his release from prison and successful integration back into society, he co-founded the Fraud Discovery Institute. The company investigates fraud, and has literally uncovered hundreds of millions of dollars of fraud and has assisted law enforcement in shutting down these illegal investment schemes. Minkow's success in investigating fraud is likely a result of his ability to think creatively and look for unconventional ways to find evidence of fraud.

A look at all the potential sources of information in Chapter 5 makes it clear that a fraud investigator has plenty of options for investigating a suspected fraud. It all comes down to persistence in looking for ways to tie together individuals and companies.

CHAPTER 7

Investigation of Asset Misappropriation Schemes

A sset misappropriation schemes are the most common fraud schemes perpetrated against companies by their employees. The theft of assets can be divided into three major categories:

1. Cash receipts schemes are designed to steal the money that is coming into the company.
2. Cash disbursement schemes focus on theft of money that is going out of the company or on fraudulently causing money to go out of the company for the fraudster's benefit.
3. Noncash schemes include the theft of valuables other than money from the company.

This chapter starts the process of walking through the various fraud schemes and how they occur, discussing the ways companies can decrease their exposure to these frauds, and illustrating fraud investigation techniques that will uncover the various types of schemes.

Cash Receipts Schemes

Skimming

Schemes that involve the skimming of money are very difficult to detect, investigate, and ultimately prove. These types of schemes are carried out before money is recorded in a company's accounting system. Because of this "off-book" nature of the crime, little or no trail is created for investigators to follow.

Skimming happens at the point of entry of money into a business. The gatekeeper who receives those funds is the most likely person to steal the money. Typical jobs that might involve access to funds in this way include bank teller, waitress, store cashier, salesperson, or medical billing clerk. Hundreds of jobs could afford someone an opportunity to skim funds from a company, but these common examples illustrate the ease of theft but the difficulty of investigation.

Imagine a case involving a waiter or waitress who takes an order from a customer, which includes an appetizer, a meal selection, and a beverage. The customer receives all the food and pays for all the food, but the server has not entered the appetizer into the cash register, and instead pockets that part of the customer's payment. This is a simple example of how easy a skimming scheme can be carried out.

It is easy to see how this could happen. Instances like this are probably less common in restaurants that use computerized systems and have good controls in place. A restaurant might require that the kitchen not release any food that is not in the computer, with management actively supervising employees to be sure that this rule is followed. That can be a pretty effective control and would go a long way toward preventing skimming by waiters and waitresses. But what about a restaurant in which no controls like this are in place? It would probably be fairly easy for the servers to run a scam like this. How would anyone ever prove it? Unless the waiter or waitress is caught in the middle of the act, how could restaurant management later prove a theft of this nature? It would be very difficult.

In a retail environment, an investigator will look for clues that skimming might be occurring. Telltale signs from cash register data might include excessive voided transactions or no-sale entries. These can be legitimate things that happen during an employee's shift, or they can be done to make it appear to the customer that the employee is ringing up a sale, while she or he is really stealing the money. By comparing the instance of these void or no-sale transactions between employees and shifts, you may find one employee has an alarmingly high rate.

In an office setting, the process of skimming is usually a little more difficult. Suppose a customer goes to the phone company and makes a cash payment at the window, but does not bother with a receipt. The cashier could easily take this money without entering anything into the record-keeping system, thereby accomplishing a theft by skimming. The customer has no proof of payment, and neither does the phone company, because a receipt was not generated. However, this creates a problem. If the customer's account is not adjusted to reflect the payment made, the customer will likely complain when the next bill is received in the mail. So although the cashier was easily able to steal the money before it was noted in the accounting system, a red flag of fraud will likely be raised soon unless the customer's records can be adjusted soon.

The customer may be out of luck without a receipt, but too many customer complaints like this would create a red flag that might alert management to a fraud. Yet imagine how difficult an investigation would be. There is literally no documentation related to the theft. Unless an employee is caught in the act, a fraud may be very difficult to prove. This type of situation emphasizes the need for segregation of duties to prevent fraud in the workplace. If the processes of receiving payments and recording payments in the accounting system are separated, the chance of theft decreases dramatically. The cashier could steal the payment, but if she or he has no ability to update account records to conceal the theft, there is less chance the theft will occur.

Skimming schemes can be carried out in numerous ways, and detecting and preventing them varies from industry to industry. No matter what industry a company is within, it is important to develop surprise audit procedures that would uncover a skimming scheme. If you were going to steal money before it enters the accounting system, how would you do it?

If you managed a large apartment complex, maybe you would rent out a couple of the apartments without filing the paperwork in the office. You would collect the rent from those tenants but pocket it, with the property owner never being the wiser. As a fraud investigator, it may be your responsibility to brainstorm how a situation like this could be prevented. How about a regular audit of the allegedly vacant units? Someone who is not responsible for the money and doesn't have a chance to steal is required to verify vacancies and submit a report on them. That report is then compared to rent collections and the total rent expected from the property. The person in charge of collecting rent could no longer secretly rent out an apartment and keep the proceeds, because the other employee's vacancy report would tip off the owner.

Because skimming is so difficult to detect and prove, companies should rely heavily on preventive controls. If employees think they are being actively monitored, they are less likely to steal. Effective tools in the fight against skimming could include:

- Video cameras to monitor employee activities
- Active involvement of managers
- Involvement of customers by alerting them to the company's policy to issue a receipt for all transactions
- Segregation of duties to eliminate opportunities to cover theft
- Surprise audits or counts to deter fraud

So how would you investigate a case of alleged skimming if it is so difficult to investigate things leaving little or no paper trail? Some ideas include:

- Look for obviously altered or incorrect documentation.
- Examine accounts for irregular entries, especially high-volume, low-balance accounts like miscellaneous, voids, cash over/short, write-offs, returns, and the like.
- Look at accounts receivable aging reports to identify irregularities. Unusually old balances might be signs of skimming that wasn't followed by an adjustment to a customer's account.

- Use trend analysis to look for patterns in accounts. Are write-offs increasing compared to account balances? Are discounts unusually high? Is a particular employee recording more write-offs, refunds, or discounts than the other employees?
- Use audit software that can quickly examine thousands of records to look for irregularities in entries or balances. The irregularities might include who is making entries, what accounts are used, or suspicious dollar amounts.

Cash Larceny

In contrast to cash skimming schemes, larceny schemes involve the theft of funds that are already recorded in a company's accounting system. This could include theft from a cash register (after all sales have been recorded) or theft from a bank deposit. Because the funds have already been recorded somewhere in the company's accounting system, in order to carry on a larceny scheme for a period of time, action must be taken to conceal the theft. This might include something like entering a false refund into the cash register, voiding a transaction, or booking an adjustment in the accounting records.

Cases of larceny come to light when cash receipts fall short of what is reflected in the accounting records. But if a case of larceny is being covered up, what techniques might be used to find clues to its existence? Larceny can be detected by using techniques similar to those detailed in the Skimming section. One common additional clue to larceny is the destruction of business records. In skimming schemes, we saw that the destruction of records probably is not necessary, because funds are stolen before a paper trail is created on the company's books and records.

Larceny schemes are different, because they deal with theft of assets that are already recorded in some way, so destruction of records could be a viable option for covering the theft. Missing records could be a sign of larceny, so any detection of missing documents should be investigated further. The examination may conclude that something was misplaced or inadvertently lost if it is an isolated incident. If the problem of missing records is more widespread, it should be cause for concern.

An analysis of a company's accounting records with auditing software could reveal some of the following red flags of larceny:

- High number of cash shortages for a particular employee, especially when there are many instances of small discrepancies
- Unusually high number of void, credit, or adjusting transactions
- Unusually high instances of employee discounts or returns

Check Kiting

One old fraud scheme is check kiting, which involves writing and depositing checks back and forth between two or more bank accounts owned by the company. The name of the game is "playing the float," or using the time between the day a check is deposited and the day it actually clears the bank.

For example, an employee steals $5,000 from bank account B, but wants to cover it up. He writes a check for $5,000 from account A, and deposits it into account B. This covers the original theft, but the fraud could quickly be discovered due to this unauthorized check written out of account A, which must be covered up as well. A check for $7,000 is then written from account B and deposited into account A. This ensures that the original $5,000 check from account A will not bounce, and adds $2,000 of phantom money to the scheme. The fraudster then has to cover that check, so he writes a $10,000 check from account A, to be deposited into account B. As the scheme goes on, the timing of the deposits continues to be critical and the amounts of the kited checks grow. The typical fraudster uses checks of larger amounts to increase the amount of theft.

As electronic banking has become more widespread, the amount of time for a deposit to clear has been decreased. This makes kiting schemes much more difficult to pull off. A thief can no longer be assured of having a couple of days to cover her or his tracks. It is quite likely that deposit details will be transmitted electronically overnight, and that is usually not enough time to allow a check kiting scheme to flourish.

Check kiting schemes are usually very easily detected by examining a company's bank statements. It is clear that several checks going back and forth between an organization's bank accounts is cause for concern. Many fraud investigators have seen kiting schemes that have generated 50 or 100 or more checks per month moving between accounts. These situations could have been detected with a simple review of the bank statements and canceled checks.

Disbursement Schemes

Devising and executing a cash disbursement scheme using expense report theft, check tampering, fake vendors, shell companies, or pay-and-return schemes is not difficult in a company with holes in its vendor and accounts payable systems. All of these methods cause the same end result: The victim company pays money to a party it should not pay, because of a charge that did not benefit the business, products or services that were never rendered, or an inflated charge.

Expense Report Theft

A very common asset misappropriation scheme is the theft of funds via expense reports. Many employees find it is not too difficult to manipulate the system in a way that inflates their reimbursement. Some employees are blatant about their theft, double-expensing items or adding phony tips or cash payments to their expense reports. Others are a bit sneakier about it, stretching the limits of business-versus-personal expenses or altering numbers on a receipt to increase a reimbursement.

Many companies do not strictly enforce ethical standards related to expense report items because of the amount of time and effort it takes to examine all the details of expense reports. There are two basic ways to steal via expense reports: (1) misuse of the company credit card and (2) false reporting of cash expenses on requests for reimbursement.

Common expense report theft schemes include:

- Claiming items that do not qualify under the reimbursement policy, and concealing the true nature of the expenses to ensure they are approved.
- Reporting multiple expenses just below the threshold requiring receipts. Many companies have a lower limit of $25 or $50, and all expenses below these amounts are not required to be supported with receipts. Employees can take advantage of this by inflating smaller expenses just up to the receipt limit or by claiming completely fictitious expenses that are also below the limit. Larger expenses may also be split so as to avoid receipt requirements.
- Double expensing of items, often achieved by charging something on the company-paid credit card, and then submitting the receipt separately to obtain a cash reimbursement. Double expensing can also occur when an employee has a duplicate receipt for a meal, and submits that one after the original receipt was already reimbursed.
- Expensing personal items as if they were business expenses. This is easily accomplished with purchases from an office supply store, as those charges could be legitimate business items. Expensing personal vacations as business trips is also a risk.
- Creating phony expense items to generate a cash reimbursement.

Expense report theft is often detected only through a detailed examination of reports, receipts, and other supporting documentation. It may require access to company calendars to determine whether an employee worked on certain days or was traveling on company business. An old-fashioned examination of the reports will require the detailing of dates, amounts, and payees. It will be important to cross-check cash reimbursements to any credit card charges paid directly by the company.

Travel charges must be checked to ensure that expenses paid directly to a travel agency by the company are not expensed a second time. Does the company have a policy against using a credit card for travel charges, in favor of booking all accommodations through an approved travel agency?

Wide-scale examination of expense reports for many employees or over extended periods of time is probably not practical. The details of a specific case will help dictate the appropriate level of examination. Ideally, an employee or small group of employees can be isolated for examination of their expense reports. It is appropriate to conduct testing on only a sample of expense reports. If this is done, it is important that the particular expense reports or line items that are tested appear to be representative of the employee's expense activity. For example, if a period of five years is under examination, it is going to be important to make sure some expense reports are selected from each year, and that the ones selected appear to reflect a "normal" amount of activity (rather than selecting reports with unusually high or low activity).

If a certain time period is of particular interest, it is best to include those expense reports as additional testing. For example, if you're examining five years of data, but are aware of one three-month period that is suspicious because of other information gathered in the case, the investigator should select normal periods for testing from each of the five years and then examine the expense reports for that three-month period in addition.

Companies can reduce their exposure to expense report fraud by implementing a system of predetermined expense allowances. They might provide a set daily per diem for meals, as well as an additional fixed cash allowance for incidentals. In this case, it is important to verify the dates of travel and the adherence to the guidelines. Some companies use computer software to monitor expense reports and look for unusual activity. Clearly, results from that software should be carefully examined, and the expense reports in question should be investigated if this is relevant to the current fraud examination.

Personal Purchases with Company Funds

A variation on expense report theft is directly purchasing goods or services for personal use with company funds. Executing the fraud is simple. The employee just needs to get an invoice into the company's system and make it appear as if the goods or services were for the benefit of the company (even though they were not). Schemes like this are easier when the employee uses a vendor that the company regularly uses and pays. An invoice from a known vendor is likely to receive less scrutiny than one from a vendor the company has never paid.

If a company has the same person in charge of authorizing purchases and authorizing payments to vendors, this type of fraud is even easier. There is no cross-checking of whether goods or services really benefited the company. In contrast, if a purchasing agent has secured goods for his personal use, that might be uncovered if another employee is in charge of authorizing payment of invoices. When others are involved in examining documentation, it is less likely that an employee will engage in fraud. If she or he does try to commit a fraud, there is a greater chance of it being discovered early.

Schemes of this type can be initiated in several different ways, including:

- Falsifying purchase orders and signatures
- Exceeding authority in executing purchase orders
- Altering legitimate existing purchase orders

To detect a scheme using company funds for personal purchases, the investigator should:

- Examine documentation for evidence of an unusual mix of items purchased from a supplier, which could suggest some personal purchases.
- Look for anomalies in the address to which products or services were delivered.
- Be on the lookout for suspicious or altered documentation that might be intended to conceal a theft.
- Search for unusual instances of missing documentation, which might be a result of a fraudster destroying the proof of theft.

Register Disbursement Fraud

Employees can commit fraud via the cash register by engaging in schemes to issue false refunds or by falsely voiding sales. False refunds, overstated refunds, or false void transactions are simple attempts at covering a cash theft from the register. If done successfully, the refund or void will cover up money missing from the drawer, and at the end of the shift, the register will balance.

In any case, there should be a well-defined procedure for processing a refund or void, with proper supporting documentation required. For example, a voided sale should require a copy of the original invoice to be taken to prove that there was an actual sale to void. Inventory on-hand should agree with the records following the void. Manager approval of voids or refunds may also decrease this type of fraud.

Detecting register disbursement fraud can be done by employing some of the following procedures:

- Notify customers that receipts should be issued for all transactions, and that store management should be contacted if a receipt is not received.
- Examine voids and refunds by employee, looking for unusually high rates of voids or refunds for certain employees.
- Verify documentation in support of voids or refunds to determine whether proper approval was secured.

Check Tampering Schemes

Check tampering is a scheme in which an employee alters or forges a check for her or his own benefit, or intercepts and fraudulently converts a check from the company to a third party. In both cases, the employee is committing fraud via a disbursement scheme. A dishonest employee can carry out a check tampering scheme in one of four ways: authorized maker, forged maker, forged endorsement, or altered payee.

Authorized maker schemes are the most difficult check tampering schemes to prevent and detect. In this type of fraud, an employee with the proper authority to sign checks writes checks for her or his personal benefit. Obviously, the difficulty lies in that the person creating and signing checks has authority to do so, and therefore the checks will likely not look unusual to the casual observer.

It is easy to say that the way to prevent an authorized maker from issuing checks for personal benefit is to restrict her or his access to blank checks. That may help, but common sense says that the check signer is a management member who may easily exert control over subordinates. Those subordinates could be intimidated into making out checks for the fraudster's benefit, or into handing over blank checks. This illustrates the importance of monitoring any controls that are put into place and giving employees a way to report intimidation or suspicions of fraud. Override of controls by management is one of the biggest fraud risks a company can face; therefore, monitoring and enforcing them across the board is necessary.

A forged maker scheme is carried out by forging the signature of the person authorized to sign checks, either by signing the person's name or by using a signature stamp without approval. There are multiple ways to forge signatures on a check, and technology has definitely helped with this process.

Businesses must be aware that banks are not in a position to check every signature on every check, so the skill of the fraudster does not have to be high. Remember that it is the company's responsibility to examine the bank statements and canceled checks (or check images) each month and immediately report suspicions of fraud to the bank. Most of the time, if a check fraud is not reported within 30 to 60 days of the closing date on the statement, the bank will assume no responsibility for the fraud.

A forged endorsement occurs when a dishonest employee intercepts a check to a vendor or other third party and converts the check by signing the endorsement line. A forged endorsement can also occur if a third party sends a check to the company, an employee intercepts it, and the employee forges the company's name on it. The endorsement is not difficult to do, but negotiation of the check at a bank may cause a problem. How does the thief get the bank to cash or deposit the check in her or his account? It may take only a bank employee who is not observant. If the bank teller is alert, the thief may need to establish an account with an appropriate name so that the payee on the check matches the name on the account.

Sometimes the employee makes the negotiation of the check easier by altering the payee. The thief intercepts a check and changes the payee to her or his own name, or the name of another person or company. Now there is no need to forge an endorsement, because the check can be negotiated in the name of the altered payee. Common tricks used to alter payees include using erasable ink in the original preparation of the check, with the intent to alter it after management has approved and signed it, using correction fluid or some other manual means to cover the original payee and replace it, or having management sign a blank check and then inserting an unintended payee.

Many check tampering schemes could be prevented with some basic controls:

- Safeguard blank checks and monitor access to them.
- Restrict the access to signature stamps and check-signing machines, and carefully monitor any use of them.
- Create rules for the custody of prepared checks that have not yet been signed.
- Prohibit check signers from handling blank checks.
- Utilize the bank's positive pay service, which will match checks known to be written against the bank account each day against those that were cashed. Discrepancies can be quickly identified.
- Separate the jobs of preparing and signing the checks so that one employee cannot do both with no oversight.
- Never sign blank checks, which are too easily misappropriated.
- Consider requiring dual signatures for checks over a certain amount.
- Have reconciliation of bank statements done by someone who is not involved in preparing, signing, or sending checks.

Some common ways to detect check tampering problems include:

- Look for out-of-sequence checks, which might indicate that someone has accessed check stock and stolen checks out of order in an attempt to conceal the theft.
- Examine checks payable to cash and manual disbursements.

- Pay attention to complaints by vendors that they haven't received payments for their goods and services, suggesting that a check to them may have been intercepted.
- Search for what appear to be duplicate payments, as one check could have been stolen and the second issued to make up for it.
- Regularly examine canceled checks (or digital images of the checks) to verify payees and endorsements, and compare them to information recorded in the check register.

Shell Company Schemes

Fake vendor schemes, also called shell company schemes, defraud companies by getting them to issue unearned payments to vendors. The fake vendors issue invoices to the company for products or services never delivered or provided, and if the company's controls over vendors and accounts payable are weak, it might be quite easy to receive a payment for those invoices.

It is often easy to get payment in this manner when the company is involved with a large or lengthy project, one with inadequate controls over the finances. Imagine a company engaged in a large computer conversion, which requires several consultants to provide custom programming and data migration services. Might it be easy for a fake company to be started, invoices to be issued related to the computer project, and to have them successfully make it through the accounts payable system? Unfortunately, the answer for some companies is "yes."

The person in a company who approves invoices for payment is at risk for approving fraudulent invoices. That is why the company needs to have additional controls in place to make sure that a fake vendor is not paid. One basic step is to prohibit payment of invoices to any company not on the "approved vendor list." The person actually approving invoices should not be able to add or delete names from the approved vendor list. By separating these two functions, the risk of fraud is reduced. Even if the person approving payment could get an invoice into the system, payment could not be approved or issued if the vendor was not on the list.

A shell company scheme could also insert an intermediary into a company's transaction in order to overcharge the company and keep the profits. Suppose Jones & Co. has an agreement with Vector Corp. to pay $1.20 for each part it buys. The purchasing manager at Jones realizes that prices for that part frequently go up and down, and that management is not diligent in scrutinizing how much was actually paid. The purchasing manager creates an entity on his own called Smith Inc., which will now be the supplier of the part to Jones.

Smith actually pays $1.20 for the part from Vector, but sells it to Jones for $1.25 each. The purchasing manager and his shell company, Smith, have added no value to Vector. They have merely caused Vector to pay $0.05 more than it should for each part it needs. Imagine if Vector is ordering hundreds of thousands of those parts at a time. The losses could mount quickly. This is the simplest example of what a shell company pass-through scheme looks like. In reality, there may often be several interconnected shell companies all used in conjunction to defraud another company.

It is easy to see how such a scheme can be successful. Companies are buying thousands of different materials and parts to make their products or perform their services. The prices of those inputs might frequently change, and companies rely on their purchasing managers to provide honest services and get them the best possible prices for those inputs.

Detecting Billing Schemes

A billing scheme like check tampering or a shell company scheme could be detected with some of the following techniques:

- *Analyze disbursements*, looking for many large, round amounts, or amounts falling just below a threshold that requires additional approval for payment.
- *Look for unusually large expenses, unexplained variances in expenses between years, or expenses that exceed budgeted amounts.* Billing schemes may inflate expenses enough to cause one or all of these comparisons to yield questionable results.

- *Examine the financial statements for variances in expenses that should track predictably with revenue.* Cost of goods sold is a popular account in which to conceal theft via billing schemes because of the high level of activity in this account. If the account varies significantly from expected values when compared to revenue, however, this might indicate a billing scheme.
- *Cross-check addresses of employees and vendors*, looking for exact matches or close matches.
- *Compare vendor addresses to mail drop address databases* to check for businesses that may not have a legitimate location.
- *Examine invoices for suspicious data.* Are invoice numbers consecutive, such that it looks like the vendor is issuing invoices only to your company? Is there suspiciously little detail on the invoices? Are there obvious typos? Is basic company information like phone or fax number missing?
- *Verify ownership of vendors that are suspected shell companies.* While many fraudsters will use fictitious names to disguise the ownership of the shell companies, sometimes real names are used and can offer clues in cases of suspected fraud.
- *Look for signs of legitimate business for the purported vendor.* Are they in the phone book? Do they have a website? Is there evidence of other customers? Do they exist as far as anyone else knows?
- *Collusion between employees will make such schemes much more difficult to detect.* Normal checks and balances that are carried out by multiple employees may be thwarted if those employees decide to team up to commit fraud.

Verification of the validity of a vendor is not terribly difficult. One of the easiest ways to find out whether a vendor really exists to do legitimate business is by simply checking the phone book. Legitimate vendors are typically listed in the white and yellow pages, and this is made easier by online white- and yellow-page listings. Look for a business registration with the city, county, or state. Find out whether the vendor is incorporated, who is listed as the registered agent, or whether a DBA filing ("doing business as") has been made. Check court records for any evidence of the existence of a real company.

Consider contacting companies in the same industry as the company for whom you are investigating to find out whether they have knowledge of the vendor or have done business with the vendor. Simple procedures like visiting the address on file or using an online service to see a map of the area, or possibly even zoom in for a street-level view of what is at the address on file, can provide important information.

Vendors might also be verified through a service like Dun & Bradstreet (D&B), which maintains business credit history information. Access to their records is available for a fee, and a history of doing business with other companies will help verify that the vendor in question is a bona fide company. The absence of a credit history with D&B should not necessarily be considered proof that a vendor is phony, however. Many small businesses simply have never established an account with D&B, as their business may not need one. It is important to use the absence of a credit profile in conjunction with all other available information to determine the legitimacy of a vendor.

Pay-and-Return Schemes

Establishing a shell company to overbill one's employer is risky, and involves some work in order to minimize the chance of discovery. One alternative to a shell company is a pay-and-return scheme, in which an employee causes a legitimate vendor to be overpaid for products or services rendered. The employee might alter the invoice to cause the company to pay more than is really owed, or create a scheme to double pay legitimate invoices, or cause a vendor to be paid when an invoice has not even been submitted by the vendor.

In any case, a legitimate vendor ends up with more money than it should have. The employee then arranges for the vendor to return the excess funds to the company. The returned money is intercepted by the dishonest employee, who keeps the money for her or his own benefit. You can see how easy it could be to get away with a scheme like this.

The vendor is legitimate and probably has no reason to suspect that its returned payments are being intercepted. Personnel at that company probably accept that mistakes occur occasionally, and they are not troubled by the fact that their company was overpaid. They are all too happy to correct the error by returning the money.

If the employee committing the fraud is careful enough, the victim company will probably never suspect that invoices are being altered or fraudulently entered into the accounting system. As long as the employee does not get too greedy and cause expenses in certain accounts to get too far out of a normal range, no one will suspect a fraud.

Although these examples all assume that the vendor is not an accomplice to the fraud, this type of scheme can also be carried out with a vendor who actively participates in the fraud. In this type of case, the vendor would likely return payment to the employee, who would agree to split the proceeds with the dishonest vendor. This could be considered a type of *kickback* scheme, discussed in more detail in the next chapter.

Prevention of these schemes can best be accomplished by segregating the functions of purchasing products and services from vendors, authorizing payments to vendors, and distributing payments. Vendors should be instructed on the "official" way to return overpayments to the company, and should be advised to contact management if asked to return payment in any other way. Incoming mail should never be delivered directly to an employee involved in accounting functions. A separate employee (or the mailroom) should receive and inspect all mail in order that any payments coming in the door can be immediately recorded.

A pay-and-return scheme could be detected with some of these techniques:

- Analyze disbursements, looking for unusually high disbursements to specific vendors.
- Look for duplicate invoice numbers or invoice numbers that occur out of sequence, which could indicate a manipulation of invoices by an employee.

- Search for duplicate dollar amounts, which could suggest the double payment of an invoice.
- Examine variances in expenses between years and between budget and actual, which might uncover unusually high disbursements.

Payroll Fraud

Inflating hours worked, benefits earned, or pay rates are some of the most common and straightforward ways of committing payroll fraud. Manual timekeeping obviously creates more risks for overstatement of hours worked. Computerized timekeeping systems make manipulation more difficult, although not impossible.

Paid leave time is ripe for abuse, because so many companies simply do not have procedures in place to prevent employees from taking time off but getting paid regular wages for that time, instead of using their sick leave or vacation time. It is not uncommon for employees to use paid leave during a week but then get paid overtime hours later in the week, even if their actual work hours haven't exceeded 40 hours. Controls should be in place to flag these instances and prevent them.

In a properly controlled environment, a supervisor would be required to sign off manually or electronically on the hours worked by employees. Failure to verify the hours or weaknesses in the sign-off process allows fraud to occur at this point in the payroll function. It is, of course, possible for a supervisor to collude with an employee to inflate her or his payroll. It is harder to detect a fraud in which employees are colluding, especially when a management member is involved. The parties to the fraud are going to jointly cover up for each other, and that will make many frauds difficult to find. Random checks by people outside of the payroll or supervisory function may help cut down on collusion. If the supervisor knows that auditors are going to periodically test the records and look for irregularities, she or he may be less likely to engage in fraud.

Ghost employees are an age-old type of internal fraud, in which a perpetrator has a nonexistent employee receive a paycheck from the company. The ghost employee might be a real person who cashes the check at her or his bank with no problems, or the ghost employee could be a fictitious person altogether, requiring a little more work in order to cash the paycheck.

In theory, it should be difficult to issue a paycheck to someone who is not an employee. In an environment with good controls, an employee could not be added to the accounting system without proper documentation and authorization by one or more levels of management. These controls are aimed at determining that the company has hired a real person, for an authorized position, at a proper pay rate, and in the proper department. However, not all companies follow such procedures to verify the existence of the employee and the job. In many cases, it is relatively easy for a payroll processor to add someone to the payroll, and as long as the amounts do not get too large, it can go undetected for a long time.

Ghost employees could be detected at the point of payment if a company had the right procedures in place. Requiring direct deposit of payroll checks discourages ghost employees, because it creates a verifiable paper trail that is often easier to trace than with paper checks. If a company is insistent on using paper checks, it is advisable to make employees receive checks in person, to reduce the risk that a fake employee could receive a check. Payroll records and personnel records should be maintained by different people or departments. The personnel department should verify any changes to payroll, and new hires should be verified through reference checks and background checks.

Commission and bonus schemes are centered around inflating sales figures so that compensation that is based on company revenue is also increased. By creating fictitious sales or by causing sales to be recorded early, an employee can receive higher pay. Commissions are often paid as a percentage of sales, and bonuses can be calculated in a similar fashion, although sometimes they are also based on whether a certain threshold is passed.

The detection of payroll fraud schemes will largely be based on a detailed examination of records to determine whether hours and pay rates are being properly recorded and paid. Other procedures that can help detect payroll schemes include:

- Examine payroll records in detail to verify the existence of employees.
- Look for missing data in payroll records, such as missing social security numbers or addresses, which could indicate ghost employees.
- Search for employees with unusually low income tax withholding, suggesting the potential for a ghost employee with a scheme to make the net paycheck as high as possible.
- Examine and verify all pay rate changes for the year.
- Look for anomalies in overtime pay, specifically looking for employees who have unusually high overtime compared to others or as a percentage of base pay.
- Conduct occasional audits of paychecks, including both leave pay and overtime pay, looking for instances of improper overtime pay.
- Compare budgeted payroll to actual, looking for unusual variances.
- Examine commissions and bonuses paid as a percentage of revenue, looking for unusual variations.
- Inspect aged receivables by salesperson or other commissioned employee, to determine whether old unpaid balances are more frequently related to one or two employees.
- Review uncollectible accounts receivable to determine whether any of the sales may have been fictitious and related to a payroll scheme.
- Look for unusual spikes in sales for certain regions, salespeople, or product lines, which could be related to a payroll fraud scheme.

Payroll Tax Theft

One common way to cover a theft of money from a company is by stealing payroll tax deposits. A company is expecting money to go out a couple of times per month for federal and state payroll taxes, so it is not too hard for a fraudster to cut himself a check for a like amount, but then not remit funds to the taxing authorities. Sometimes payroll tax theft schemes are more elaborate, and they take some sleuthing to unravel. Likely scenarios include:

- Overpay the regular payroll tax deposits, and at the end of the year, the fraudster includes that overpayment as payroll taxes withheld on her or his own W-2, and gets the overpaid amounts refunded to herself or himself.
- Remit payments to the government, but have them applied to the fraudster's personal account as estimated income tax payments. Management still sees the payments clearing with the IRS or state, but the business never gets credit for the amounts.

Often, the employee ensures that the payroll tax forms are filed, but no payments are made. This is risky, however. Once the IRS becomes aware that payroll taxes are due, notices may be mailed to the business, and the perpetrator risks discovery. If the employee instead fails to file the payroll tax return while also not sending in payment, there is no telling how this will affect the chances of discovery by the IRS. Sometimes the business immediately receives a notice that the returns have not been filed. Other times, the company slips through the cracks, and notices aren't sent by the IRS for months or years.

The simplest way for a business owner or executive to see whether payroll taxes are being paid is by examining original bank documents. If the taxes are paid via electronic funds transfer, then a look at the bank statement should confirm that the government really got the money. If payments are made by check, then examining canceled checks or digital images of checks directly from the bank should help confirm the payments. When fraud is suspected regarding payroll taxes, it is imperative to take the next step and contact the Internal Revenue Service and the state taxing authorities to get official information about what has been reported and paid.

No matter how the fraud was perpetrated, it is important to get information from the taxing authorities about payments made, so the company can quickly determine whether there are amounts outstanding. Interest and penalties mount quickly on unpaid payroll taxes, and although the IRS may negotiate in the case of an employee theft, the company should pay amounts due as quickly as possible to decrease its financial exposure. The best way for a company to protect its payroll taxes is to use a reputable payroll service to prepare all payroll and associated taxes. The opportunity for theft of payroll tax deposits is significantly decreased this way.

Noncash Schemes

Equipment and Inventory Thefts

The theft of physical company property is not necessarily difficult to get away with, and many people are surprised to learn that schemes to steal equipment or inventory do not often involve a lot of covering up. Part of the reason such a theft may be so easy is that equipment and inventory normally are moved throughout the company's building during a workday. Who is going to realize that items are being moved so they can be stolen?

The other reason it is so easy to steal these items is because management trusts its employees, and in order to do their jobs, they need access to these things. Items of greater value are often locked away or closely monitored, and the employees with access to them are generally highly trusted. Often no one suspects that they would ever steal. Items can also be shipped to fake customers so that items appear to be leaving the company legitimately. Asset transfers between plant and warehouse locations also offer the opportunity to conceal theft.

The theft of raw materials or finished goods is sometimes not hard to cover, especially if a company has poor inventory tracking systems. If management has no idea how much of a particular item is supposed to be on hand, logically there is no real way to prove theft of that item. Preventing the theft of equipment or inventory requires good record keeping and regular verification. Taking regular inventory counts will help reduce the amount of theft, because would-be thieves know that someone is watching. Restricting access to areas holding valuable assets is important, and computerized systems (with barcodes or keycard access) can track who is accessing these areas. Security cameras and security guards can also help prevent asset thefts.

The following procedures can detect inventory or equipment thefts:

- Count and reconcile items on hand to the inventory and equipment records.
- Look for unusually high or low inventory balances, as well as negative balances, because theft of these items can be the root cause of unusual balances in the accounting records.
- Carefully scrutinize inventory adjustments, which might be used to conceal theft.
- Examine unusually high instances of write-offs or adjustments to customer balances, which could be related to a theft of outgoing items.
- Determine whether customer complaints related to nonreceipt of goods allegedly shipped are a result of theft of outgoing items.
- Look for alteration of shipping and receiving documentation that may be used to cover a theft.
- Examine discrepancies between invoices and receiving documentation to determine whether there was a theft of items received.
- Review old accounts receivable balances to determine whether they could be related to a theft of outgoing inventory or equipment.
- Examine records related to restricted area access.

Misuse of Assets

Employees use company resources for their personal benefit on a regular basis, and some of it is sanctioned by the employer. Things like using computers and Internet access, "borrowing" office supplies, making copies, utilizing long distance telephone service, and using company equipment are often overlooked. The typical use of these items is minor and therefore not really worthy of investigating.

The use of company assets is a privilege that can be easily abused by employees, and companies should create clear guidelines about acceptable use. When the monetary value of the use of the assets becomes significant, employers are more likely to crack down. One common way to abuse company assets is by using them for an employee's "side venture." This could be relatively minor and include occasional computer or telephone use, or it could be very serious, to include things like using company vehicles and equipment.

Maybe the most vulnerable company asset when it comes to an employee's independent business venture is the employee's time. What happens if the employee is suddenly spending hours on a telephone or computer solely to conduct business for the side venture? And what happens if the employee's business conflicts with the interests of the employer, whereby they end up competing for business? Companies can and should have policies in place about these types of conflicts of interest, but they may still occur. Management should be wary of sanctioning employee use of company assets, because it can become difficult to draw a line between acceptable and unacceptable use.

Detecting the misuse of company assets is really dependent on the active monitoring of employees and the company's systems. Regular enforcement of the company's policies relative to employee use of company assets will tend to decrease the instance of misuse and, accordingly, monitoring efforts can probably be reduced as well.

CHAPTER 8

Investigation of Financial Statement Fraud

The manipulation of a company's financial statements does not occur as often as asset misappropriation schemes like payroll fraud, check kiting, or inventory theft. However, financial statement fraud schemes are much more costly than other types of fraud. Some may wonder what the losses in a financial statement fraud could be. After all, the employees involved are just manipulating numbers on paper, but there is really no harm to anyone, right? Wrong.

Financial statement fraud is so expensive because its effects are far-reaching. Just a few of the many effects of financial statement fraud include:

- Bank offers a loan that is riskier than it believed.
- Stock price becomes inflated.
- Company pays higher bonuses than it should.
- Executives issued more stock options than they deserve.

Banks can be stuck with bad loans they never would have made if they knew the true financial situation of the company. Investors buy stock they might not otherwise have bought. Employees get bonuses and perks that are higher than they should be, and the company has a lower ability to pay those bonuses based on the true numbers.

When a financial statement fraud is finally uncovered, millions or billions of dollars stand to be lost by interested parties. Investors want their money back. Banks call loans. Customers stop doing business with the company. Employees lose jobs because of reduced revenue. The outlook of the company looks worse, and all of these negative effects snowball until, many times, the company is put out of business.

Companies that are likely candidates for financial statement fraud, sometimes referred to as *earnings management*, are ones that appear to be doing significantly better than other companies in their industry. There is always an industry leader, and there is always a possibility that a particular company has a much more efficient operation than competitors. But more often, industry conditions affect all the players in a similar fashion. A company that has jumped ahead of all others in the industry with a much higher level of profits can be engaged in financial statement fraud. The better the financial results are compared to the bulk of the companies in the industry, the more skeptically the financial statements should be viewed.

This chapter examines the broad categories of financial statement fraud schemes, red flags that investigators should be looking for, and investigative techniques to ferret out the fraud.

Revenue Overstatement

The first and most common way that financial statement fraud is carried out is through revenue overstatement. The easiest way to improve the apparent financial condition of a company is by fraudulently inflating revenue. Companies can do this by:

- Booking fictitious sales
- Holding the books open at the end of a period
- Recognizing legitimate sales early
- Shipping items not ordered by customers and booking the sales
- Booking revenue before it has been earned on projects in progress
- Recording sales for items produced but not yet shipped, or only partially shipped

- Booking sales but delaying shipment to customers (bill-and-hold schemes)
- Not properly recording allowances for returned goods

Revenue overstatement is detected by examining revenue patterns and looking for irregularities. Unusual changes in cost of goods sold might signal a problem, as companies that book fictitious revenue do not always book corresponding expenses. Revenue overstatement may also be suspected when a company has consistent cash flow problems, even in light of apparently increasing sales and profits.

One irregularity that may not often be considered as such is a suspiciously constant increase in sales or profits from period to period. Remember that especially for public companies, there is a high expectation that revenues will grow by a certain percentage, and that profits will increase accordingly. Executives know the "acceptable" parameters for their numbers. Anything outside those ranges will raise questions. So it is not a stretch to believe that revenue and expenses could be manipulated to conform with those expectations.

For example, I examined the financial statements and related notes for a public company that sells a specific type of clothing. The financial statements showed extremely stable gross profits as a percentage of revenue. Yet the notes to the financial statements indicated that the business was suffering because of significant increases in the cost of materials. Therefore, it would make sense that the gross profit percentage might be negatively affected, unless the company could raise the retail pricing enough to cover the cost increases. Independent evidence suggested that retail prices were not up, bringing into question the accuracy of the profit-and-loss statement and raising the possibility that the numbers were manipulated.

This situation illustrates a common occurrence in cases of financial statement fraud: The face of the financial statements appears reasonable. The fraud is discovered only once facts are cross-checked with the numbers and outside evidence is compared with management's assertions.

Other indicators of fraudulent manipulation of revenue include: existence of unusual ratios related to inventory or accounts receivable, rebooking receivables so unpaid amounts related to phony sales do not look so old, or recording large write-offs shortly after the close of a period. An internal report (a tip from an employee) of revenue manipulation may be necessary in order for auditors or other professionals to become aware of the fraud, as schemes to manipulate revenue are often carefully crafted and covered up.

If a revenue overstatement is suspected, the following procedures can be used to investigate:

- Examine the books for adjusting entries, especially toward the end of an accounting period, that increase revenue.
- Look for "on-top" accounting entries that were booked after the close of the accounting period and changed the financial statement numbers.
- Examine documentation to determine whether sales toward the end of an accounting period were legitimate. This is often referred to as *cut-off testing* by auditors.
- Search for transactions toward the end of an accounting period that cause the company's results to barely meet or exceed budgets, projections, or Wall Street's expectations.
- Compare purchase orders to invoices to see whether a customer issued a purchase order after a sale was booked. The purchase order could be proof that a sale was booked before the items were even ordered by the customer.
- Analyze write-offs and returns in later accounting periods to see whether earlier sales may have been improperly recorded.
- Look for altered documentation that may indicate backdating of sales documents.
- Check post-closing shipping documentation to determine when goods were actually delivered to customers.
- Use date-stamped and time-stamped evidence like e-mails, faxes, and accounting system entries to try to determine when agreements were made, contracts were signed, and sales were actually made.
- Compare commissions paid to sales booked. Management is not eager to pay commission on fictitious revenue.

- Examine payments of invoices to determine whether payment lags on sales booked toward the end of an accounting period. Delayed payment may suggest the sale was not really made until later.
- Independently confirm sales dates and amounts with customers.
- Independently confirm accounts receivable balances with customers.
- Examine what appear to be partial payments on accounts, which could suggest inflated invoices used to manipulate revenues. The customer clearly would pay only what is legitimately owed, making it appear as if there has been only partial payment.

Channel Stuffing

Channel stuffing (also known as *loading* in some industries) is a particular type of revenue manipulation in which companies offer large discounts, extended payment terms, liberal return policies, or other unusual incentives to encourage customers to buy products earlier than they otherwise would. This harms the company in two ways: It means the sales are far less valuable because of the concessions made, and it also means that sales in future periods will be hurt, because customers are presumably purchasing now what they would have bought later.

At times, this practice may be a legitimate strategic initiative through which the company attempts to secure sales that could possibly go to competitors if they waited. This strategy may also be employed if the company wants customers to stock up for seasonal needs. It might also be part of a marketing strategy for the brand or an attempt to make a big move among competitors. But if the channel stuffing is a legitimate strategic initiative, the company will disclose it along with the impact it may have on future sales. There are no rules against offering customers incentives to buy, but it is necessary for management to disclose these incentives when they are likely to have a large negative impact on future periods. When channel stuffing is actively concealed, it is cause for concern.

Undisclosed channel stuffing is done when management is desperate to boost revenue in a particular period. One common reason is the inflation of revenue to make the company look more attractive to a potential buyer. The risk here is obvious: The buyer purchases the company based on revenue numbers it probably considers normal, only to find out after the close of the purchase that not only were the revenues not normal, but there is going to be a huge drop in revenue in future periods because of the channel stuffing.

One widely known case involving channel stuffing was Sunbeam Corp., under the direction of turnaround specialist Al Dunlap (known to many as Chainsaw Al). The Securities and Exchange Commission (SEC) charged former officers of Sunbeam with "a fraudulent scheme to create the illusion of a successful restructuring of Sunbeam and thus facilitate a sale of the Company at an inflated price." Part of the scheme was accelerating sales that would have occurred in later periods, without disclosing that future sales would suffer as a result of this.[1]

Signs of channel stuffing include increased revenue and shipments toward the end of a period or irregularities with inventory storage, balances, and reserves. Cost of goods sold may rise as a percentage of revenue during the time when channel stuffing is happening. Methods of investigating channel stuffing are similar to investigating the other types of revenue manipulation already discussed in this chapter, with a focus on determining whether special pricing or special terms applied to the sales.

Round-Tripping

Round-tripping is another method of fraudulently inflating revenues. The concept is pretty simple, although the execution may be complex. Companies round-trip by recording transactions that have no economic benefits but help inflate revenue. Quite simply, the company recognizes revenue and an offsetting expense. The net effect on the profit-and-loss statement is zero, but the scheme is employed to increase the top line for a company whose financial statement users demand ever-increasing revenue.

This practice has been common in energy trading and telecommunications. Companies have resources to sell, and they find buyers who turn around and sell those resources right back to the original company.

Each company, in effect, increases its revenues but has an expense of a similar amount. This results in no net profit to either company, but each company receives the benefit of a higher top line. This obviously differs from a normal business transaction, in which each company independently decides to purchase products or services from the other without this swapping. There is a clear intent in setting up a round-trip arrangement, and that intent to fraudulently inflate sales figures is the problem.

Indicators of round-tripping include an unusually complex structure for a sale, difficulty in tracing funds that should be received or paid in conjunction with a transaction, and missing or concealed details about the true rights and obligations of each party to a transaction. This type of fraud is investigated using the procedures explained in the revenue overstatement section of this chapter, with a special focus on examining documentation related to the revenue and expenses that will confirm that funds were not exchanged or that the transaction did not include a normal independent purchase on the part of either party. The most common round-tripping schemes happen between companies in similar lines of business, so transactions between these companies should be scrutinized more closely.

Asset Overstatement

Enhancing the balance sheet is a common financial statement scheme, and asset overstatement is one part of it. Increased assets make financial ratios look better and generally make a company look stronger and more attractive.

Improper valuation of *investments* can fraudulently inflate a company's assets. The risk generally lies in classifying the investments correctly. They can be classified as trading, held to maturity, or available for sale. Each of these classifications requires a different value to be shown on the balance sheet. Management may be unwilling to record a write-down for unrealized losses, and may therefore try to misclassify an investment to avoid that. The classification may also change if management is interested in recording a gain.

It is popular to overstate *accounts receivable*, especially since bank lending decisions are often heavily influenced by the strength of a company's assets. *Inventory* is another area of the balance sheet that is ripe for fraud, because it is so easy to get away with. Inflating inventory also has a positive impact on profits, making it even more desirable. If inventory is overstated, cost of goods sold is understated, and therefore profit is overstated. Schemes to inflate inventory values include overstatement of quantities on hand, overstatement of the value of inventory items, and improper capitalization of costs to inventory.

Overstatement of the quantity of inventory on hand involves reporting more items on hand than are actually there. The false journal entries may be supported by phony shipping and receiving documents and invoices, and possibly by empty boxes stored in a warehouse. It is common knowledge that outside auditors perform a limited number of tests on inventory, so inflating the value of inventory on hand is not all that difficult. Auditors typically inspect the inventory at only a small number of locations, even if a company has many warehouses. Their inspections are often incomplete. Even if their inspections meet the professional standards to which auditors must adhere, there is still a relatively small amount of verification of inventory done.

Sam Antar is the former CFO of Crazy Eddie who pleaded guilty to federal charges of fraud in the securities case that blossomed out of a massive fraud and the eventual bankruptcy of the electronics retailer. His tales of fooling the auditors in charge of verifying inventory are legendary, and they include "helping" the auditors with test counts, making changes to audit work papers that were left relatively unsecured at the Crazy Eddie offices at night, and fabricating paperwork to support the inventory valuation.

It is easy to see how auditors could be fooled by phony documentation or empty boxes in a warehouse, which cannot all be examined. Signs that an inventory fraud might be in progress include:

- Inventory at locations at which access is restricted, denied, or otherwise impossible

- Increases in inventory at locations company management knows will not be subject to physical examination by auditors
- Insufficient or nonexistent documentation to prove the existence of inventory
- Unusual patterns of shipping and receiving, especially ones that result in large increases of inventory toward the end of the accounting period
- Excessive movement of inventory between company locations with insufficient recordkeeping
- Large differences in inventory test counts
- Unusually large quantities of high-value items on the books
- Reversing entries booked to inventory accounts shortly after the close of an accounting period

Fraudulent inventory counts can happen many different ways, and it is not necessarily difficult for management to succeed with one of these schemes. Fraudulent inventory valuations are even harder for auditors and investigators to find and prove. It is difficult to prove that a company did not write-off obsolete inventory or did not create a proper reserve for inventory with a reduced value. Red flags of inventory valuation schemes include low or nonexistent inventory reserves, few write-offs of obsolete inventory, and the apparent ownership of similar items of inventory from year-to-year without any write-offs or allowances.

The more progressive an industry is, the bigger this issue may be. For example, the technology surrounding personal computers changes quickly. It stands to reason that a manufacturer of computers might regularly have write-offs or write-downs due to the quick changes in the industry. If there were no such adjustments to inventory values, it would seem suspicious.

Improper capitalization of costs to inventory is a process by which costs such as sales, administrative, advertising, and other costs are not expensed but are booked to the inventory cost. This creates two problems: The inventory balance is overstated on the balance sheet, and expenses are understated on the profit-and-loss statement. It is important to examine what costs a company is charging to inventory, and make sure that they are adding to the inventory balance only the amounts directly related to producing that inventory.

Recording nonexistent *fixed assets* can inflate a balance sheet and is desirable because it increases an asset class that may be borrowed against. Fixed asset values are also propped up when a company records less depreciation in a period than it should.

When fraud related to fixed assets is suspected, the investigator should:

- Examine fixed asset records looking for a legitimate business purpose for the items.
- Physically inspect fixed assets to verify their existence.
- Look for assets that might need to be written down or written off.
- Verify the cost on the books with purchase documentation.
- Examine depreciation for evidence of using inappropriate lives or methods.

Assets with impaired values should be written down, and this applies not only to fixed assets, but also to other assets like goodwill, trademarks, patents, and other intangible assets. These are undeniably difficult manipulations to detect, because often the process of valuing such assets is complex and involves judgment on the part of management.

In general, investigators looking for evidence of asset overstatement should:

- Examine adjusting entries, especially toward the end of an accounting period, that increase assets.
- Look at periods following the accounting period in question to see whether reversing entries are recorded, suggesting that the original accounting treatment was improper.
- Look for entries of large, round numbers that may suggest manipulation of financial statements, especially when such transactions occur toward the end of an accounting period.
- Look for trends in asset balances and unusual items that fall outside normal trends.

- Trace assets back to supporting documentation to verify their existence and cost.
- Examine skeptically any capitalization of items other than fixed assets, looking for a motive to reduce current period expenses. Do not accept explanations at face value, and instead demand authoritative guidance that proves such capitalization is acceptable.
- Be suspicious of altered or missing documentation, particularly when it relates to accounts or transactions that are already deemed questionable.

Liability and Expense Understatement

Lowering a company's liabilities and expenses creates an obvious and immediate improvement to the financial statements. The lower the company's debt, the stronger its financial position and the better the financial ratios look. One simple tactic to reduce the liabilities on the books is to make an adjusting entry lowering liabilities and increasing equity.

Liability and expense accounts are easily manipulated, and often this fraud is more difficult to detect than revenue or asset overstatement. An investigator looking at revenues and assets is examining what is already there, to determine whether it should have been excluded during the accounting period. In contrast, an investigator examining liabilities and expenses is trying to find something that should have been recorded but is not there. She or he is searching for something that may or may not exist, and there may be no real proof one way or another.

Imagine asking management to provide supporting documentation for items like this: The investigator sees a $1 million sale toward the end of the year that looks suspicious and asks management to provide documentation related to the sale. Management could refuse to provide the documentation or say that it does not exist, which would cause the sale to appear even more suspicious. Alternatively, management could provide the documentation and the investigator could independently determine whether the sale is legitimate.

In contrast, how does the investigator examine the liabilities and expenses? Suppose the fraud investigator believes that an additional $2 million of expenses should have been recorded during the accounting period. There are indicators that accounts payable are unusually low, so the investigator asks management to provide documentation of the additional expenses. Management says, "There are no additional expenses."

Now what? How does the investigator even begin to look into something like that when she or he cannot yet prove its existence? The difficulty in investigating cases of suspected liability or expense understatement is clear. It is not impossible, however, and in this chapter we will talk about some of the ways those suspicions can be confirmed.

Understating *accounts payable* can occur by not recording invoices from vendors in the proper period. This could be accomplished by closing a period early on the payable side, preventing employees from entering additional accounts payable into the accounting system, even though items should have been recorded.

In a similar way, management could understate *accrued liabilities* like wages, benefits, and property taxes to avoid booking an expense and to reduce liabilities. To find evidence of understatement of accounts payable or accruals, the investigator should look for unusual patterns in recording payables and accruals. Of particular concern is a low level being recorded at the end of a period, followed by higher than normal amounts shortly after the close of that period.

One of the key procedures that is most effective in detecting unrecorded accounts payable or accrued liabilities is the examination of periods **after** the one in question. By examining what was paid after an accounting period closed, the investigator may come upon items that should have been recorded earlier. Traditional auditors also use this technique during annual financial statement audits to find unrecorded expenses or liabilities, and they refer to this as *cut-off testing*. Be aware, however, that the volume of testing in this area by traditional auditors may be low, and a fraud investigator should do sufficient testing to substantiate liabilities and expenses.

Management may also favor *capitalizing expenses* instead of properly expensing them. This means an increased profit, and it also inflates assets. One option is capitalizing expenses to costs of inventory, discussed earlier. But in general, it is common to see capitalization of expenses to fixed assets. One reason this is done is because it is so easy to conceal. Fixed asset balances are often large, especially in manufacturing companies that own buildings and significant equipment.

There are common arguments used when trying to defend capitalization of expenses, namely that these costs are "investments" that are intended to benefit future periods. In the minds of managers trying to justify financial statement manipulation, they may argue that it is most appropriate to match the future revenue that will be realized from these "investments" with the expenses. Management's solution is to defer the expenses to future periods, but this argument does not usually meet the requirements of the accounting rules.

A company often does not capitalize large amounts all at once, because large amounts might draw the scrutiny of auditors, and these flimsy arguments may have to be used. Instead, management will likely start capitalizing smaller amounts, which have a good chance of going unnoticed. But if this goes on for any period of time, the capitalized total can be huge.

This type of fraud was carried out at WorldCom. Management was purchasing companies rapidly and was quickly increasing its expenses related to providing telecommunications services. Revenue was not keeping up with the costs, so executives came up with the idea of capitalizing "line costs." When this practice was detected by internal auditors, management argued that since the telephone lines were not generating revenue now, they were an investment. When the lines started generating revenue in the future, expenses could be charged against them, and the revenue and expenses would be properly matched. This was clearly a violation of accounting rules and part of what led to the uncovering of an $11 billion fraud at WorldCom and the company's ultimate demise.

Unearned revenue is an important liability account, as it often represents the fact that a company has received money or value from a customer but has not performed its obligations to the customer. The liability is shown on the balance sheet to signify that the company still has an obligation to someone. Failing to record such a liability is essentially the same thing as recognizing revenue early, which was discussed earlier in this chapter.

Moving liabilities between *long-term and current* liabilities is a tactic aimed at improving financial ratios and adjusting the financial statements depending on the configuration of liabilities that is most preferable at the time. Ordinary consumers might not consider this a true fraud, so long as the company has recognized all liabilities on the financial statements. But in fact, intentionally misclassifying those liabilities between current and long-term is a fraud.

Failure to record liabilities, such as warranty reserves, service obligations, or contingent liabilities (such as the money that likely will be lost due to a lawsuit), is an obvious risk. Management might suggest that these items cannot be recorded because there is not a reasonable possibility of loss or the potential loss amount cannot be estimated properly. Often these are obvious tactics used to avoid recognizing liabilities.

To detect liability and expense understatement:

- Examine payables and debts to look for balances that appear too low.
- Analyze adjusting entries at the end of a period to determine whether all accruals have been made, or whether there were last-minute adjustments that appear to enhance the financial statements.
- Look for unusually low expenses, especially cost of goods sold (as those often have a predictable relationship to revenue).
- Examine accounts related to purchase discounts, write-offs, or other adjustments, which could signal an attempt to lower liabilities.
- Analyze expense accounts related to payroll, benefits, rent, property taxes, interest on loans, and the like to determine whether they are unusually low, potentially signaling a failure to record all accruals.
- Look for significant assets purchased without corresponding debts recorded.
- Determine whether lease liabilities have been recorded in accordance with lease contracts.
- Examine documents in support of revenues, such as contracts or sales agreements, to determine whether revenues are being recognized before they have really been earned.
- Analyze warranty and service claims histories to determine whether current accruals are reasonable compared to historical figures.

- Look for evidence of warranty or product liability issues that may require accruals. Such evidence might be found online or in newspapers, as defects or problems with products are sometimes reported there.
- Skeptically examine pension liabilities to determine whether proper amounts have been expensed.
- Examine invoices from outside counsel to identify matters that may give rise to contingent liabilities.
- Search court records for evidence of legal cases, insurance claims, matters with the SEC, or issues with auditors that may require recording contingent liabilities.
- Be on the lookout for documentation that is obviously altered or curiously missing.
- Analyze entries and account balances after the close of the period in question, to determine whether there are unusual adjustments or higher-than-normal expenses that might indicate items that should have been recorded earlier.

Evidence of understatement of liabilities or expenses is often analytical in nature. The analysis of such items requires significant judgment, and documentary evidence of this type of fraud is difficult to obtain. That should not deter a fraud investigator, however, because the risk of financial statement fraud using these methods is high.

Reserve Manipulation

Companies are required to book reserves for a variety of things, including accounts receivable, sales returns, warranties, inventory obsolescence, litigation reserves, and more. Some of the biggest reserves may be booked when a company is discontinuing a line of business or otherwise restructuring. Creating a reserve requires a great deal of judgment by management. They must create a proper balance in the reserve account based on what they think will happen in the future. Auditors rely on management to calculate reserves fairly, but only time will tell whether their estimates were correct.

Manipulation of reserves is a common financial statement fraud, and often it is not detected. Accountants often refer to reserves as a "cookie jar," into which management can occasionally dip. If a reserve is too low, expenses in the current period will be understated, and earnings will be inflated. In the future, the company will have to recognize higher expenses to make up for the inadequate reserves.

The flipside of the reserve problem is booking larger reserves than are necessary. If the company is having an exceptionally good quarter or year, the company may be able to afford to book a higher reserve. Then in later periods, if profits are suffering, it can reverse some of those reserves to prop up earnings.

Detection of reserve manipulation is extremely difficult. An investigator could look at actual expenses in later periods and compare them to the original reserves. However, that does not necessarily mean the original reserves were right or wrong. The reserves could be completely reasonable on the date they were calculated, but down the road more information may become available or things may change, and the reserve will be impacted.

Misrepresentation or Omission of Information

The notes and disclosures included with financial statements can be misrepresented, inadequate, or nonexistent. This type of fraud impacts the financial statement user's ability to fully evaluate the numbers. It is difficult to detect, however, because these disclosures do not directly impact the financial statements and cannot be discovered with analytical procedures performed on the numbers.

Typical misrepresentations or failures to disclose include:

- Pending litigation or government investigation (e.g., an inquiry or investigation by the SEC or the Food and Drug Administration)
- Potential product liability or significant warranty issues
- Significant events such as changes in product offerings or services, or downturns in the market demand for a company's products or services

- Obsolescence of technology being used by the company, especially if the company has historically relied on that technology to drive revenue
- Decline in the market value of significant investments held by the company
- Changes in accounting rules or their applications that may mean numbers between accounting periods are no longer comparable
- Existence of related party transactions or agreements that may not have been negotiated at arm's length
- Events occurring after the close of an accounting period (subsequent events) that might have a material impact on the opinions of financial statement users

The best way to identify misleading, inaccurate, or incomplete disclosures is to compare the disclosures with the financial statements and determine whether the story fits. Look for inconsistencies between what is said in the notes and what is shown in the financial statements. If there is reason to believe that management is not being candid, or that the accounting rules are not being followed, or your intuition says other things are not right, a more in-depth examination of the financial statements is likely warranted.

Improper Recording of Mergers and Acquisitions

Improperly recording the amounts attributable to mergers or acquisitions or improperly classifying amounts from these transactions is yet another way to manipulate a company's financial statements. Such manipulations may be made in an attempt to inflate asset values (e.g., record market value instead of book value) or lower periodic expenses related to the transaction (e.g., assign an asset class that offers a longer depreciation period).

Reserves created during the acquisition process can be manipulated as well. The issue of reserve manipulation was discussed earlier in this chapter, and the application here is the same. Companies may set up reserves at the time of acquisition to account for some costs that will be incurred during the process of integrating the two companies. There could be anticipated losses related to discontinuing a particular product, selling off a certain unwanted segment of the business, or elimination of redundant jobs.

If an insufficient reserve is booked, future periods could be negatively affected when expenses are incurred. Management could also purposely book a reserve that is too large, with the intent of using the excess reserves to smooth earnings in future periods. Users of the financial statements might not object to large reserves, because they are often accepting of the fact that costs come along with acquisitions. Management knows this and might use the opportunity to book a little extra and save it for later when profits from regular operations fall short.

Off-Balance-Sheet Items

Companies might attempt to use off-balance-sheet financing to avoid recognizing certain items on their financial statements. Special-purpose entities can be used to legitimately meet an economic objective or transfer risk from the company to the outside entity. They cannot be used just to hide things that otherwise would be required to be reported on a company's financial statements.

The best example of the abuse of special-purpose entities is the case of Enron. These vehicles can be used legitimately, but the area is ripe for abuse if management insists on covering up a poor financial position or enhancing a good financial position. That is exactly what Enron executives did. They hid liabilities in the special-purpose entities and used them to make large, undisclosed payments to related parties. These acts eventually contributed to the downfall of Enron.

How is fraud via off-balance-sheet items to be detected by a fraud investigator? It is very difficult. Management often goes to great pains to hide the existence of these entities when they are being used to facilitate financial statement fraud. An investigator will likely have to rely on an insider tip about such entities, or may otherwise come across a tiny clue about their existence.

A fraud investigator should stay on the lookout for changing business relationships or disappearing debt. Why has one of the company's major customers appeared to have changed the way they do business with the company? Why has there been a significant change in the amount of business they do with the company? Why have certain liabilities been wiped off the balance sheet? Why are debts disappearing, even though increasing operations would normally mean that additional debt is required?

Accounting Involves Judgment and Estimates

One of the most challenging parts of putting together accurate financial statements involves the use of estimates. So many variables go into these estimates, and the process is not one-dimensional. Complex calculations involving estimates far into the future are involved, and it is often difficult to challenge the validity of the calculations or assumptions.

Take, for example, an account like warranty reserves. This balance sheet line item is only an estimate of what management thinks will have to be paid out in the future for warranty claims. Because it involves the future, it stands to reason that the number is only an estimate. Many variables could affect the estimate, and who is to say how heavily each variable should be weighted? It could involve current sales volume, past rates of warranty claims, changes in products that may increase or decrease future claim rates, the legal environment of the company's industry, changing government regulations, and more.

Complicating the process of estimating financial statement line items is the fact that these items almost never stop moving. As business is continuously moving and changing, the financial statement estimates are changing as well. Because these items involve the judgment of management and seem to be a moving target, how can an investigator determine whether a line item was fraudulently manipulated? This is a difficult question to answer, and the answer involves judgment as well.

One measure of the reasonableness of an estimate may be the actual financial results long after the financial statement date. A comparison will show how well management estimated the item. Yet even if the estimate and the actual result are far apart, that does not necessarily mean a fraud occurred. The estimate has to be analyzed in light of the information that was known at the time the estimate was made. An examination of the financial statements, then, must focus on whether the numbers were objectively reported. Earnings management—the act of manipulating the numbers to present financial statements that conform to management's desired numbers—is ultimately difficult to prove.

Earnings Management

Financial statement fraud sometimes is referred to by the less-menacing phrase of *earnings management*. Apparently, if we use nicer-sounding words, the crime is not as bad. And in the minds of many, earnings management really is not fraud, anyway. But that is not true. When management is trying to "manage" earnings, it means they are manipulating the financial statements to achieve some predetermined result. There is no denying that this is financial statement fraud.

Investigators should not let a renaming of financial statement fraud deter them in their work. It appears that public company investors and government regulators will tolerate a certain level of earnings management before action is taken. That is not the concern of the fraud investigator. If you are asked to investigate an instance of fraud, and your analysis reveals financial statement fraud, it is your job to report it. No "acceptable" level of financial statement fraud really exists in the world of fraud examiners. Either fraud has occurred or it has not. The job of the fraud investigator is to report those facts objectively.

Note

1. SEC Press Release 2001-49, May 15, 2001, www.sec.gov/news/press/2001-49.txt.

CHAPTER 9

Investigation of Corruption Schemes

In general, corruption schemes include bribery, kickbacks, extortion, and conflicts of interest. These types of schemes involve a payoff in return for some sort of advantage or preferential treatment, an undisclosed relationship that nets a party a financial or operational advantage or favor, or an attempt to force certain preferential action to be taken.

Corruption schemes deprive companies, their owners, and employees of honest services and make it impossible for companies to compete fairly in the bid process or earn all of the profits to which they are entitled. When an employee or associate is taking money off the top of a transaction or compromising a company's process, the harm is more far-reaching than she or he probably realizes.

Fraud involving corruption is extremely difficult to detect, because most, if not all, of the actions related to these crimes occurs "off books." There is no paper trail to be discovered when someone is handed bribe money in a dark alley somewhere. A receipt is certainly not given, and the person accepting the bribe is not going to report that money to the employer.

Bribes

The detection of bribes is difficult because they occur outside the accounting system, and they are related to legitimate business transactions. Consumers often think of government scandals related to bribery, but plenty of bribes take place in the private sector as well, and very likely these crimes occur far more often in private businesses.

Bid-rigging is a type of bribery scheme in which a vendor is given some sort of advantage in what is supposed to be a competitive bidding process. One vendor may be given insider information to help win the bid, or a vendor may have already been secretly selected, with a phony bidding process set up to ensure that this vendor "wins" the bid. An employee may also rig the process of bidding for a contract by crafting the specifications for bids so narrowly that only one vendor will "qualify" to bid.

There could also be a scheme to get a company to buy more from a bidding vendor than necessary, with internal employees fraudulently affirming things the vendor says the company needs, when it really does not. Vendors might also collude in the bidding process, making agreements between themselves that essentially control who bids and inflate the bid prices.

Bid-rigging can be detected by recognizing an unusually high contract price. If there are a low number of bidders in conjunction with this, suspicion should be even higher. Look for unusual bidding patterns or an apparent collusion, based on the similarity of information in the bids. A vendor with a track record of winning contracts with bids submitted at the last minute and by very slim margins might indicate that an employee is supplying that vendor with information about the other submitted bids.

Instances of bid-rigging might not be detected until well into the project. Excessive change orders that increase payments to the contractor should be examined skeptically. This could indicate that the bidder purposely bid very low to win the contract, with a promise from an employee to get changes to the contract approved, thereby increasing the vendor's compensation.

When bidders who were not awarded a contract later appear as subcontractors on the project, it might indicate collusion in the bidding process. It is possible that the bidders agreed to divide the proceeds of the contract in exchange for each doing certain portions of the work.

Kickbacks

A kickback occurs when a company overpays for goods and services, and a vendor gives part or all of that overpayment to the perpetrator. It is often not difficult for a purchasing employee within a company to engage in a kickback scheme, which is why it is so important for a company to put good controls in place. Anyone who has the authority to award contracts or purchase products or services on behalf of the company is at risk for engaging in a kickback scheme. Other employees involved in the process of approving a contract, such as production managers, engineers, or quality control supervisors, are also at risk for receiving kickbacks.

One of the best ways to detect a potential kickback scheme is through data analysis. Software can hunt down irregularities in pricing or quantities, and can analyze the frequency of purchasing from vendors. A higher than normal cost of raw materials from one or more vendors or an unusually high volume of purchases from one vendor can signal a problem.

The quality of raw materials or merchandise should be monitored closely. It is not uncommon for a supplier to substitute inferior goods in order to make a greater profit from the transactions. The supplier has a lower cost for the inferior goods, but is charging the price of the higher-quality goods to the customer. There is an instant profit, and this is one type of fraud involved in kickback schemes. If quality issues are discovered, look into the potential for a corruption scheme.

It is important to analyze trends in spending and look for explanations for increases and decreases. Look for irregularities in inventory accounts, including excessive write-offs, which may be used to cover up for overpayments.

Contracts with vendors should include a *right to audit* clause, be-cause their records could be an important part of an investigation of bribery or kickbacks. Under such a clause, the company would have a right to look at the accounting records of the vendor to determine whether there was a fraud or misrepresentation.

Extortion and Conflict of Interest

Extortion is not nearly as common as bribery or kickbacks, but it still happens with some regularity. Whereas in a bribe, something of value is given in order to get an advantage in a transaction, extortion is a scheme in which someone demands money or assets in order to do business together. For example, when someone at the company requesting bids demands that bidders pay a sum of money to be considered for the project, extortion has occurred.

A conflict of interest exists when an employee, executive, or owner of a company has an undisclosed economic or personal interest in a situation or transaction, which then negatively affects the company. The scheme involves some influence that the employee, executive, or owner is able to exert over a transaction. The result is harm to the company, with benefit to the employee, a friend, a family member, or some other party. In order for a scheme to be a true conflict of interest, the relation-ship or interest must be undisclosed.

Related-Party Transactions

People don't always think about business transactions with related par-ties as being part of a fraud scheme. They recognize that it may be common to do buy or sell transactions with family members, friends, related companies, the companies of family or friends, or other entities that have a special relationship with a company or its management or owners.

So long as related-party transactions are conducted on an arm's-length basis, there probably is no fraud. Arm's-length transactions are carried out in the same manner in which you would do business with an unrelated party. The same pricing, payment terms, delivery specifications, bidding process, and awarding of contracts that would apply to outsiders is used with these related parties.

The problems arise when the related parties have a special advantage in doing business with the company, especially when that advantage harms the company through reduced revenue, increased expenses, or other concessions. Related-party transactions can be difficult to uncover, especially if management is actively concealing the fact that the parties to a transaction are related. If the relationship is being covered up, there is probably some questionable aspect to the business being done.

Questionable transactions with related parties could include some of the following:

- Giving related bidders information that has not been disclosed to other bidders
- Paying more than market rates for products or services
- Buying or selling real estate at prices much higher or lower than available on the market, to the detriment of the company
- Extending credit to customers who would otherwise not be worthy of credit under the company's normal guidelines
- Writing off accounts receivable from related parties with no legitimate business reason
- Lending money at rates significantly below market rates, or interest-free
- Forgiving loans without a legitimate business reason, or giving "loans" without any intent of being paid back
- "Doing business" with a company that is little more than an entity created to make payments to a related party appear as if they were legitimate business expenses
- Paying for goods and services that are never rendered to the company
- Engaging in "consulting agreements" in which parties are paid sums of money but do not provide any real services to the company
- Failing to disclose related-party transactions in accordance with applicable accounting rules

■ Actively concealing the existence of relationships that might cause others to question whether a transaction is being conducted with a related party

   Uncovering related-party transactions is difficult, especially when there is active concealment of the relationship. Investigators should be looking for:

■ Unusually high prices for products or services.
■ Write-offs of account balances that are abnormal.
■ Unusual consulting payments to vendors.
■ Loans or other transactions that do not have any apparent business purpose.
■ Evidence that the company is funding another business entity.
■ Details of transactions that appear abnormal, such as an unusually low price paid by a customer.
■ Complex transactions that do not need to be complex; sometimes the complexity is used to hide the true nature of the transaction and/or the parties.
■ Public record providing information on large customers, vendors, or consultants, looking for undisclosed relationships. (See Chapter 5 for more information on searching and using public records.)

   Doing business with related parties is not necessarily wrong. In fact, doing business in a way that benefits a related party (to the detriment of the company) is not always wrong, either. It depends on the disclosure of the relationship and the nature of the transactions with the related party. Disclosure of all relevant details may cause the related-party transaction to be legitimate. Active concealment of the situation tends to suggest the opposite.

Money Laundering

Money laundering is not a fraud scheme. It is a crime that is committed to cover up other crimes, but it is not the same thing as fraud. The primary purpose of money laundering is to take money that has been received from criminal activities (dirty money) and make it appear legitimate (clean money). Dirty money can come from illegal activities such as drug dealing, prostitution, robbery, bribery, illegal political contributions, tax evasion, or fraud. The laundering process hides the real origin of the money and makes it look like it came from a legitimate source.

Money laundering has three key stages:

1. *Placement* is the stage in which the criminal introduces the money into the financial system. This is the riskiest part of the scheme, because controls have been put in place to detect money laundering activities.

   For example, banks that receive large cash deposits are required to report them to the federal government. That restricts the criminal's ability to deposit the illegal proceeds. Criminals are therefore forced to find other ways to get their money into the financial system.

   One way to legitimize dirty money is through a legitimate business, introducing the dirty money into the business as "revenue." Cash-intensive businesses like restaurants and nightclubs are popular options for this scheme. Cash obtained illegally is added to deposits from the legitimate business, and upon being deposited to the bank, all of the money now appears to be legitimate.

2. *Layering* is the part of the process by which the criminal obscures the origin of funds and reduces the possibility of detection of that origin. Moving funds between accounts, banks, financial institutions, and countries can easily obscure the origin of funds. The more transfers are made, the harder it is to trace money back to its source.

3. *Integration* is the removal of the now-legitimate money from the financial system so that it can be used by the criminal. It could be used for legitimate purchases and expenses, or it could be used to fund additional criminal activity.

Money laundering can be detected by looking for:

- Unexplained increases in cash deposits
- Increased deposits for which no customer is identified
- Unusual transfers out of a bank account, rather than typical use of funds to pay business expenses
- Frequent cash bank transactions just under the $10,000 limit for bank reporting on the Currency Transaction Report (CTR)

Foreign Corrupt Practices Act (FCPA)

The Foreign Corrupt Practices Act (FCPA) has once again become a major concern of companies doing business internationally. The Act applies to all companies based in the United States, whether they are privately held or publicly traded. The purpose is to stop companies from using corporate funds to bribe foreign officials to secure business.

While bribery is not an acceptable and legitimate way to do business in the United States, it does have its place in some foreign countries. There are cultures around the world in which bribery is a normal way of doing business and would never be considered improper. In some countries, even though bribery is frowned upon, it is a known fact that it is necessary to get business done.

The FCPA makes it illegal for any officer, director, employee, agent, or stockholder of any company to pay money, give a gift, or promise to give anything of value to a foreign official to influence any act or decision, induce him to commit a violation of law, or secure any improper advantage.[1] Yet the interpretation of this law is not so simple.

One exception to FCPA is a situation in which a payment to a government official or political party is made to expedite or secure the performance of routine governmental action. It may also be okay to give a gift or something of value if it is considered lawful in the area in which it was done. Obviously, a problem arises in an area in which a bribe or payment may not be permitted under the law, but is nonetheless common practice there.

Management must be aware of schemes to get around the FCPA. Games can be played with invoices (such as adding on extra charges) or with vendors (such as a fake vendor submitting an invoice) to conceal the true nature of bribes. In some areas, they may call payments "gifts," but they are what we would commonly refer to as bribes. It is the company's responsibility to determine whether bribes are actually occurring and whether they might be violations of FCPA.

Prevention and Detection

Because the detection of bribes, kickbacks, and other forms of corruption is so difficult, companies often find that preventing the crime is easier than detecting it after the fact. As already mentioned, off-books frauds like these are difficult to recognize, because they do not leave a paper trail within the company. They are often detected only when someone gets suspicious about rising costs without any explanation or some obscure clue arises.

Good internal controls can prevent corruption schemes from gaining traction, but only if those controls are monitored and enforced. For example, there may be a policy against a purchasing agent receiving gifts from vendors. However, if no one monitors compliance with that rule, then it is completely meaningless. Monitoring of the controls cannot be done only from the inside. Will a purchasing agent voluntarily report that he has received a large, prohibited gift? Probably not. That is why it is important to remain in close contact with vendors to communicate the company's policy to them and inquire about things of value they may have recently given to business partners.

An anonymous reporting mechanism (like a hotline) is essential for any company that is intent on preventing and detecting corruption schemes. Bribery and kickback schemes are difficult to conceal when several people are involved in the transaction. Management should make it as easy as possible for co-workers or company outsiders to report suspicions of corruption. The anonymous nature of a hotline may also encourage reporting, because it allows people to maintain anonymity if they fear reprisal.

Maybe most important in preventing these well-concealed schemes is the top-down intolerance of unethical behavior. A bribery or corruption scheme will thrive in a company and culture that generally tolerates a certain level of dishonesty. The company that is committed to taking action against dishonesty of any size has a much better chance of preventing such behavior all together.

Note

1. www.usdoj.gov/criminal/fraud/docs/statute.html.

CHAPTER 10

Investigation of External Fraud Schemes

E xternal fraud schemes for purposes of this book include any type of fraud that is not part of an occupational fraud, also referred to as employee theft, embezzlement, internal fraud, or employee fraud. We have already discussed internal fraud schemes in the chapters on asset misappropriation, financial statement fraud, and corruption schemes. The external fraud schemes are perpetrated by or against parties outside of a company, such as vendors, customers, competitors, or other parties unknown to a company and its management.

Obviously, many different schemes have developed over the years, and there is only limited space to discuss them. This book attempts to highlight some of the most common schemes and the methods a fraud investigator can use to uncover them. This chapter is not intended to be all-inclusive of the schemes or the investigative techniques. Rather, it is a starting point and a guide for a fraud examiner who is interested in some common business fraud schemes.

Corporate Espionage

Theft of or infringement upon the intellectual property or secret information of a company is the goal of corporate espionage. This type of scheme can include the theft of client lists, strategic plans, pricing plans, marketing data, confidential financial information, development information on future patents, personnel data, or other secret data that contributes to the success of an operation.

Information like this can be compromised by computer hackers who get into a company's system and steal information directly or set up nefarious software that will regularly send information to unauthorized third parties. Dishonest employees can also be responsible for leaking confidential data, taking hard copies of secret documents, or e-mailing (or otherwise transmitting over the Internet) digital copies.

Companies can become victims of corporate espionage in the most ordinary of ways:

- *Social engineering.* A thief could convince an employee that he is supposed to be let in the building, or could gather information over the phone or via e-mail by convincing someone that he's supposed to receive the information.
- *Dumpster diving.* Employees who aren't careful when throwing away papers with sensitive information might allow secret data to be available and intact for those willing to go through the company's trash.
- *False pretenses.* Someone intent on stealing corporate information could get a job with a cleaning company or other legitimate vendor specifically to gain legitimate access to the office building.
- *Viruses and Trojan horses.* With every click on the Internet, a company risks having its system infected with nefarious software that is set up to harvest information from the company servers. Without proper computer security, this would be easy for an experienced criminal.
- *Corporate identity theft.* Use of a company's credit, business information, or reputation without management's knowledge.

Detecting corporate espionage may require assistance from people with specific expertise. Computer-based risks require the assistance of a computer security person who can help a company monitor systems for unauthorized access and track what employees are doing with data. Physical security experts may be needed to help address risks from apparently legitimate vendors who do nefarious things. Management needs to actively monitor a company's credit accounts and government registrations for any unauthorized activity.

In general, a company needs to aggressively monitor its intellectual property and other assets that are susceptible to infringement and theft. It is in management's best interest to make sure the company is asserting its rights and taking action against internal and external actors who will compromise the integrity of the assets.

Investment Schemes

Despite the proliferation of information available about phony investment schemes and the dire warnings given regularly by news reporters, consumers continue to become victims of these scams in no small number. The perpetrators of investment schemes dream up stories explaining their unusually high rates of return on money, and get people to invest with them.

These high investment returns typically amount to guarantees in excess of 10% per year. Often they are to the point of ridiculous, offering a 30% or 40% annual return. As a fraud investigator, it is clear to me that these offerings are bogus, because any investment that legitimately generated such returns would not be much of a secret to the rest of the world. But consumers, who are often eager to protect and grow their nest eggs, are all-too-willing to believe that this investment is the answer to their money problems.

These investment schemes are not usually terribly elaborate, but the stories about them are. In typical investment schemes, there is absolutely nothing legitimate about what they are offering. There is often a story about a wonderful investment vehicle, often with ground-breaking technology, a secret recipe, access to a niche market, or some other unusual-sounding detail. This cryptic detail allows the investment vehicle to create such high returns for investors, or so the story goes.

The unique characteristic that will supposedly earn the investors so much money is either nonexistent or does not have the significance that those selling the investment want you to believe. The people making the offering simply want to steal the investors' money and hope that they will buy into the scheme before they discover the hook is all a lie.

An *affinity fraud* is an investment scam in which the perpetrator gets involved with a close-knit group of people, often with a similar ethnic or religious affiliation. These groups of people often have a great deal of trust in one another. If the perpetrator can convince the group that she or he is one of them, or if the perpetrator can get a few key people to buy into the scheme, many members of the group are likely to invest their money.

Investment schemes can be identified by considering the following questions:

- Does the business of the company make sense in light of market conditions and your general business knowledge?
- Does the company exist because of some secret, revolutionary new process or product? If so, what proof is there that the technology or process is legitimate?
- Does the company rely on some rare gem, piece of real estate, antique, or other hard-to-find item? If so, is the investment scheme really scalable to the extent that the promoters suggest?
- Does the company's performance make sense when compared to other companies in the industry?
- What do objective third parties have to say about the company and its business? Are those things in line with what you are being told? Or are third parties suspiciously quiet about the company and its offerings?
- Is the business of the company so complicated that an ordinary person cannot really understand what it is selling or how it is operating?
- Are unusually high rates of return on the investments being marketed? Are such returns possible or probable? If such high rates of return are so easily obtainable, couldn't other companies do the same?
- Is the company guaranteeing rates of return on investments with them? Can their promises be verified in any way?
- Is the company's success dependent on exploiting a tax loophole or other government regulation? If it were possible and legitimate, couldn't more companies do so?

- Are certain parts of the business unusually secret? Is there a general reluctance to disclose key facts?
- Who really works in this operation? Does it appear to be just the owner and a few other people? Does that level of staffing make sense in light of the operations or results touted by the company?
- What is the background and experience of the principals? Do they have industry expertise?
- Have any of the principals been involved in scandals or bankruptcies? Do they have criminal records? Have they been accused of running any scams?
- Does the company have a board of directors, auditors, lawyers, and other advisors typical of a company of its size?
- Is the apparent success of the company related to a recent announcement, rather than historical financial results? Can the facts of the announcement be verified?

Pyramid or Ponzi Schemes

One particular type of investment scheme is referred to as a *pyramid scheme* or a *Ponzi scheme*. It is named after Charles Ponzi, who was believed to have developed the first pyramid scheme. In a pyramid scheme, investors are recruited with promises of extraordinary investment returns (interest) on their money. The promoters secretly have no investment strategy.

In order to pay the "returns" to the original investors, new investors must be lured into the scheme. The money from the new investors pays the "returns" to the first tier of investors, who happily tell friends and family about the wonderful investment vehicle they have discovered. Soon it is time for another "interest" payment, but this time both the first and second tiers need to be paid. A third, much larger tier must be lured into the scheme, and their money is used to pay the first and second tiers.

As you can see, this can go on only for a limited amount of time until the recruiting requirements are so huge that the scheme falls apart. Typically, the promoters of the scheme make their money by skimming money off the top from all investments that come in the door.

Multi-level marketing companies (MLMs) have become an accepted and legally sanctioned form of pyramid scheme in the United States. Their perceived legitimacy comes largely as a result of the products they purport to sell. Rather than just getting someone to invest in some intangible scheme, an MLM recruits an investor who puts her or his money into tangible products or seemingly legitimate services.

The products are theoretically supposed to be retailed to family and friends. In reality, the products are little more than a cover for an endless chain recruiting scheme. Well-known multi-level marketing companies like Amway, Herbalife, Mary Kay, and Shaklee give the impression that their real business is retailing products, and so consumers have little reason to be skeptical of them. The con is extended further, when it is suggested that those who like the products will naturally want to become a part of the company and do their own retailing and recruiting.

The reality is that little retailing to actual customers goes on, and the vast majority of product purchases are really "investments" made by members. The MLM companies cleverly institute minimum purchase requirements for each distributor or member who wishes to receive commission payments related to those they recruited into the scheme. With such a requirement, distributors end up purchasing products they do not need and cannot sell, just to become commission qualified.

Why is so little retailing of products happening in these MLM companies? It is generally believed to be a function of two things: pricing of the products and other choices available to customers. In order to pay commissions to multiple levels of the scheme, the pricing of the products must be high. The MLM tries to explain this pricing structure to the general public by claiming that its product is of better quality than other products on the market. That is often not really the case. In addition, today's consumers have many choices when it comes to purchasing products. Retail stores are abundant, and online shopping sites offer many choices and pricing options. Consumers often choose alternatives to the MLM products.

The real business in MLM companies is recruiting new distributors into the scheme. Without new distributors, the pyramid would collapse. These new distributors pay sign-up fees, purchase products and samples in significant quantities, and are often responsible for much of the financial growth of MLM companies. Once they become a part of the company, they see that the real way to make money is to recruit new members, and the recruiting scheme is perpetuated.

Yet studies of these schemes indicate that a high percentage of participants, often on the order of 99%,[1] spend more money than they will ever make through the MLM. Although these schemes are promoted as a way for an individual to own her or his own business and generate additional income for her or his family, that is most often not the case. The members typically spend far more money on minimum purchases, sales aids, samples, meetings, conventions, and the like than they will ever earn in commissions or overrides.

The turnover of participants in these schemes is high. The pyramid is in a constant state of collapse, and needs to be rebuilt by recruiting new members into the scheme. New members enter, make their investments in products, and hope to recruit people below them who will do the same.

Like the pure investment schemes discussed in the previous section, this system is not sustainable and eventually collapses. How can MLM companies stay in business for decades if there is constant collapse? New recruits readily replenish those who have tried and failed. An ever-expanding world population offers a constant stream of new participants ready to build their own pyramids, which will also soon collapse.

Securities Fraud

Securities fraud, or stock manipulation, is a scheme in which someone purposely (and falsely) influences the market price of a publicly traded stock. In a "pump and dump" scheme, a promoter who holds a company's stock may release false information that is intended to artificially inflate the price of the stock. The market responds to the news put out by the promoter, the stock price rises (at least temporarily), and the promoter quickly sells the stock for a profit.

The flipside of this scheme is the "short and distort" scam, in which the perpetrator stands to benefit when the price of a company's stock goes down. The investor who benefits this way holds a short position in the stock and releases false negative information about the company. The market price of the stock drops, and the short position is closed out with cheap stock, which creates a profit for the perpetrator.

There is constant debate about which side is wrongly influencing the price of a stock. Owners and executives of companies are accused of touting their companies and making things seem unfairly optimistic. Critics of the company are accused of publicizing false negative information and opinions on companies in an effort to harm the stock price.

Cases of securities fraud are generally investigated by the Securities and Exchange Commission (SEC), although a fraud investigator in the private sector might be called upon to aid in the defense of a person or group of executives who have been implicated in such schemes. Both sides of the securities fraud debate often suggest that the SEC does not do enough to investigate instances of fraud and does not take action often enough against those who violate securities laws.

There are probably many instances of people and companies breaking securities law, but the sad fact is that the SEC does not have enough people, time, or resources to fully investigate every allegation of fraud. They must choose which battles to fight, and that means some instances of securities fraud are never pursued or prosecuted.

Hidden Income or Assets

Divorce cases, child support matters, and tax cases often involve allegations of hidden income or assets. It is not uncommon for someone under investigation to "suddenly" become poor. A business that was once offering the owner a healthy living is suddenly supposedly losing money. A high-earning attorney suddenly receives minimal paychecks. A retail business is no longer transacted using credit cards or checks, but using cash only, and the cash mysteriously disappears.

In cases like these, it can be very difficult to prove that someone has income or assets. They often purposely do business in a way that leaves no verifiable paper trail. How can an investigator prove that there is, in fact, income being generated and spent?

A fraud investigator can do a *lifestyle analysis* to prove, through circumstantial evidence, that the target is in fact generating income from somewhere. This type of analysis requires the investigator to estimate the known living expenses of the target, such as mortgage payment, groceries, insurance, health-care costs, automobile fuel, and the like.

Some of these items will be easy to determine and may have substantial documentation in support of them. One such item may be the monthly mortgage payment, which is easily verified with mortgage company documents. Other items will have to be estimated based on any historical figures that are available, regional averages for items, or an educated estimate. For example, it is possible to estimate a reasonable level of monthly grocery expenses based on the size of a household and its geographic location. It is important to include in the known expenses things like vacations, vehicle purchases, and any other known large, one-time items.

The investigator must also total all known sources of funding. This includes the reported income (even if it is suspected of being under-reported), any known loans or inheritances, tax refunds, or gifts. The estimated monthly or yearly total of expenditures is then compared to known sources of cash. Any gap between the cash and expenses indicates the possibility of hidden income sources. This method does not give definitive proof of hidden income, but it appeals to the common sense argument that if an individual is spending this much money, it has to come from somewhere.

Another type of analysis that is very similar to the lifestyle analysis is the *net worth method*. Both rely on very similar sets of numbers but approach them from different directions. The net worth method is another way to connect the dots of someone's lifestyle to make a circumstantial determination of hidden income. This method focuses on the known assets and liabilities of a person and the changes in these assets and liabilities over time.

From public records or legitimately obtained private records, the fraud investigator assembles known purchases of real estate, automobiles, personal possessions, and other assets. Liabilities are tabulated as well, taking into account mortgages, personal loans, credit cards, and trade credit. The difference between the two is the net worth of the person. Net worth calculations are often done for multiple years, so that the changes in net worth can be tracked. In addition to the changes in net worth, the investigator must compile the living expenses of the person for the period. This is done in essentially the same way as the lifestyle analysis.

A person's change in net worth plus the living expenses for the period equal the funds required for the period. If this number is larger than the known sources of money, then a hidden source of income probably exists. Again, this is very similar to the lifestyle analysis, but some believe presenting findings in accordance with the lifestyle method is more understandable for lay people.

An *expense analysis* for a business may also give clues to the possibility of unreported income. Companies may try to conceal revenue when they (or their owners) are involved in litigation or tax matters in which reduced revenue helps their case. An expense analysis can be helpful, because often, when management is not reporting all sales, they fail to adjust the company's expenses accordingly. They often still want the tax benefit of as many expenses as possible, so they continue to report all expenses.

Most times, certain expenses in companies relate closely to sales. As revenue rises and falls, these particular expenses will also move in a predictable fashion. In a manufacturing environment, for example, commissions expense and cost of goods sold often track closely with sales. In a dental practice, lab expenses often move in relation to revenue. At a retail store, credit card processing fees are often closely related to revenue.

Suppose that the cost of goods sold at a manufacturer is usually 30% to 33% of revenue. If that number suddenly becomes 45% or 50% with no real explanation for the variance, it may signal unreported sales. The company has still reported all expenses related to the sales, and as a percentage of revenue, the expenses jump dramatically because revenue figures are artificially low.

This is not a foolproof method, but it can provide some clues about the information being reported and might help force the hand of someone who has been concealing financial information. Other expense items that should be examined because they might track well with revenue include hourly payroll, advertising expenses, travel expenses (for a service-based business), or supplies.

Asset searches may be necessary to find ownership of real estate, vehicles, boats, or airplanes that are undisclosed. Some private investigators specialize in these types of searches and have access to the most comprehensive databases. Seek out someone with this expertise to aid in the search.

Insurance Fraud

Falsified insurance claims cost the insurance industry many billions of dollars per year. Insurance companies run the risk of being defrauded through such schemes as arson for profit, false or inflated claims, or claims that disguise the true cause of the loss. Claims for loss of revenue or profits run the risk of fraud through inflation of pre-claim revenues or profits, and underreporting of revenues or profits post-incident.

Probably the most interesting type of case a fraud investigator may work on in the area of insurance fraud is a case of arson for profit. While fire experts will attempt to determine the cause of a fire, the fraud investigator will search for a financial motive for arson. A company deep in debt and facing closure may prompt management to decide that arson is the way to close the business and get some money out of it, too.

A fraud investigator should look for:

- Signs of a deteriorating financial condition, which is sometimes steady, but other times very quick
- Evidence of liens or judgments against the business or its owner
- Tax problems, especially if the unpaid taxes are sales taxes or payroll taxes, which are often more serious than other tax delinquencies
- Pending foreclosure actions or severe mortgage delinquency
- Repossession of equipment or vehicles by asset leasing companies or financing companies

- Significant downturns in revenue, especially unexpected sharp declines
- Unusually high payouts of salary, bonuses, or benefits to owners and/or executives shortly before the fire
- Failure to complete a key transaction that would have saved the company from financial troubles, such as major financing or a buyout

Often, business records will be purposely destroyed during the arson, with the business owner assuming that, without them, a fraud investigation cannot be initiated. What it really means is that the fraud investigator will have to be more aggressive and creative.

Records can and should be acquired directly from their original sources, including records from banks, credit card companies, taxing authorities, payroll service, vendors, and customers. The insurance company can require the insured to authorize the third parties to release information as part of the claims process. Cooperation (or lack thereof) on the part of the business owner may provide additional clues in determining a motive for arson.

Bankruptcy Fraud

In the United States, bankruptcy is a process by which individuals or businesses can either be relieved of their debts or be given time and opportunity to reorganize and eventually pay their debts. Bankruptcy court relies on full disclosure from the person or business involved in the filing. They must honestly report their assets and liabilities, or allegations of fraud may arise.

Some of the ways debtors may commit bankruptcy fraud include:

- Making false statements about the property, debt, or income of the person or business
- Hiding assets to intentionally conceal and shield them from the creditors
- Making a false claim against the debtor

- Receiving a material payment or asset from a debtor after a filing in an attempt to defeat the provisions of the bankruptcy code
- Transferring or concealing property in contemplation of a bankruptcy filing (hiding your assets before filing)
- Concealing, falsifying, or destroying records related to the debtor's financial affairs either before or during a bankruptcy filing
- Withholding information and records related to the debtor's financial affairs from a custodian, trustee, or officer of the court

People and corporations are also prohibited from using a bankruptcy filing to carry out or cover up a fraud scheme. If fraud in a bankruptcy proceeding is discovered after the bankruptcy matter is closed, debt forgiveness or discharge can be revoked, and the person or corporation can be ordered to pay the debt(s). It is not easy to prove fraud in a bankruptcy case, because often a lengthy period of time has passed, and the person committing the fraud has had ample time to conceal the fraud.

Note

1. Robert FitzPatrick, "The Myth of 'Income Opportunity' in Multi-Level Marketing," June 2008. Available at pyramidschemealert.org/PSAMain/news/MythofIncomeReport.html.

CHAPTER 11

Reporting and Litigation

Reporting the findings of a fraud investigation will require varying levels of detail and precision, depending on the specifics of the engagement. Yet it is fairly easy to develop a standard reporting process that can be followed by staff.

One option in some cases is providing an oral report to the client and counsel. This is not the most common way to report on the findings of a fraud investigation. However, it is appropriate in certain cases, such as ones in which legal counsel does not yet want a discoverable[1] report in the file.

The results of a fraud investigation are usually detailed in a written report. When writing a report, the fraud investigator must remember who will be reading the report. It is important to consider that even though today the report may be only for a company's internal purposes, somewhere down the road the report may be used by law enforcement or in court proceedings. So it is important to know the current audience for an investigation report, but it is also imperative to consider who might need the report in the future.

For example, your investigative results may initially be used by legal counsel to determine appropriate internal discipline for a fraudster. However, if your findings are serious enough, there may eventually be a criminal trial on the matter, and your report may surface there. Alternatively, the employee could file a lawsuit related to the termination of her or his employment, and the fraud investigator's report may be used to justify the termination.

Would you write a report differently if it were strictly for use by attorneys versus if it were to be used by a jury of lay people? I suspect you might, and that is an important thing to keep in mind when writing the report. Do your best to make that report understood by all parties who might read it in the future. The best way to craft a report on a fraud investigation is by keeping three key points in mind: First, the fraud investigator should stick to the facts when reporting findings. Second, the report should be easy to understand by anyone, even if the person is not highly skilled in the areas of accounting and finance. Third, think of the report on your investigation as a build-up of facts leading to your ultimate conclusion about losses.

Stick to the Facts

It is important that a fraud investigator be as objective as possible in carrying out her or his work, and that objectivity should show in the report. No one cares whether you liked the people involved in the case or what you thought about someone's appearance. They might care whether the suspect appeared nervous, but your personal biases or critiques are not really important.

Even when doing something as basic as reciting the background of the case, it is important that you demonstrate your objectivity. There is no need to debate parts of the case in the recitation of the background. That's for the attorneys to debate. If the recitation of the facts requires that allegations or disputed items are mentioned, the fraud investigator should make it clear that those items are disputed.

Keep It Simple

Making complex transactions easy to understand is no small task, but it is part of the job of any good fraud investigator. You can find the most earth-shattering proof of fraud, but if you cannot articulate your findings in a report that others can understand, your investigation results are not worth much.

Use graphs, charts, and tables to help illustrate your points. Even though you may not *need* a graph or chart to demonstrate your findings, consider that the reader of your report might benefit from it. Remember that people learn and comprehend in different ways, and that fact could be very important if your case ever goes in front of a jury. One juror might understand your written word best, so it is important to make the report very reader-friendly with short, well-organized paragraphs. Other jurors might understand the most by listening to your court testimony, which should support and reiterate the written report. Other jurors might be most receptive to pictures or charts that demonstrate what you have found.

It is important to create a logical flow to the report, either by working through the case chronologically or by using some other logical ordering, such as walking through it by entity or person involved. The narrative of the work completed, the conclusions of the investigators, and the evidence to support it should be presented in a fashion that builds up to the conclusion.

It is very effective to work through all the points that suggest a fraud was committed. Many times a "smoking gun" is not necessarily found. Rather, there are many small pieces to the puzzle that in their totality point to fraud. That build-up can be very important in supporting your opinions and conclusions.

Background Information

Everyone likes to develop her or his own convention to report writing, but you may find this methodology useful when wrapping up your investigation. This method has proven to be helpful in educating outsiders about the facts of the case, the evidence you found, and your opinions about financial losses.

Identify the client who retained your services, and identify the parties to the case. Give a brief description of the task to which the investigation team was assigned. Opinions vary on how detailed the background of the case should be in the body of the report. One rule of thumb is to offer just enough information so that the reader is aware of what prompted the investigation, what fraud is alleged to have occurred, and what (if anything) is being disputed in the case.

Often, the description of the fraud investigator's assignment does not need to be terribly detailed. It may be enough to say that the firm was engaged to examine financial documentation and render opinions about financial losses to the client. Other times, it may be important to offer a more detailed explanation of the assignment, especially if the investigator's work was limited in scope to certain issues, accounts, or parts of a company. In either case, it should be clear to the reader whether the assignment was broad or narrow in scope. Too many details can create something for the other side of a case to argue about, so it is best not to get bogged down in a lot of disputed facts and allegations.

Identify the period of time that is covered by the fraud investigator's analysis and any limitations on the fraud investigation team. For example, if certain documents were not produced or you were not granted access to key personnel, it is important to note that here. If you were asked to make certain assumptions, but were not allowed to test them, that is important to note as well.

The fraud investigator must be clear about what constitutes an opinion versus what was an assumption that she or he was asked to make. For example, in a disability insurance fraud case, the investigator may be asked to analyze the numbers assuming the insured can never work again. As another example, a fraud investigator may be asked to assume that a company is unable to produce a certain product going forward and analyze the numbers in light of that.

In both of these situations, the investigator is not asked to determine the truthfulness or reasonableness of the assumptions. Rather, she or he has been asked only to perform an investigation in accordance with the assumptions. That may be a very important fact as the case progresses, so the forensic accountant or fraud investigator must be sure to document that fact up front.

Investigation Procedures

Once a proper foundation is laid for the fraud investigation, the report should move into the investigative procedures and the investigator's findings. This is the portion in which there may be a detailed discussion of the documents examined, witnesses interviewed, and investigative techniques performed. The description of these things varies considerably from case to case. In general, you will likely describe the accounting system and the transactions you examined. The fraud investigator will describe the work of examining the evidence and tabulating or cross-checking numbers. Use good judgment about the level of detail included in your work. It is not necessary to list every document that was cross-checked. Rather, it is important to give a general overview of the procedures performed.

It is important to carefully explain calculations that were used to arrive at conclusions. This should be done in the simplest manner possible, because the report may ultimately be used by people with little or no accounting experience. Any estimates that were used during the investigation should be carefully explained and supported. What was the methodology? Why was that selected? Why is it reasonable? Where did you get the numbers for your estimates? Why are they reliable, in your opinion? How might a change in your estimate affect your final conclusions?

As you are working through your detailed explanation of your work and conclusions, remember that visual aids can help support your methodology and can assist readers in understanding your conclusions. For example, consider a case in which a company is claiming it lost revenue because of your client's actions. You have looked at detailed sales records and see that sales actually went up during the time they have claimed there was a decrease. In addition to writing a paragraph about this increase, you may also want to provide a table showing a summary of the numbers. You may further clarify the issue by adding a graph that clearly demonstrates the sales increase. By explaining this conclusion with three different tools (narrative, table, chart), you have increased the chances that a wide variety of readers of your report will understand and accept your conclusion.

Avoid industry jargon in a report unless it is absolutely necessary in order to understand some of the work or evidence. If you have to use technical terms or jargon, be sure that you have explained exactly what those terms mean in the context of this case. For example, it may be necessary to discuss accrual basis accounting versus cash basis accounting, and how these affect your opinions. These are not commonly understood terms, so it will be necessary to clearly define them and differentiate between them.

Always think ahead to the potential for a case to end up in the hands of a jury. The jurors may have no experience with accounting issues or with fraud issues. How will you get them to understand what you have done and what your conclusions are? For this very reason, your report should be written as simply as is practical. Never assume that the readers of your report have a working knowledge of accounting, finance, or fraud.

Opinions

The opinion section of a fraud investigator's report is the place in which the findings are summarized. The body of the report has already alluded to or stated outright the evidence that has been uncovered in the performance of the fraud investigation. In this section, the results should be summarized. It is best to walk through a summary of the proof, line by line, in an organized and simple fashion. A fraud investigator should not give an opinion that a person or entity is guilty or not guilty of a crime. Rather, the evidence should speak for itself.

For example, it is generally enough to say that a check was issued to an unapproved third-party vendor without proper authorization, demonstrate who was involved with that unauthorized check, explain the details of the third-party vendor (especially if it is a case of a shell company scheme), and provide copies of documents that support these facts. The reader of the report should have enough information to conclude whether this activity was improper, and then can decide whether this is indeed fraud.

If you can ascribe a degree of certainty to your opinions, you should do so. For example, a forensic accountant might state: "These opinions are stated to a reasonable degree of accounting certainty." Such statements are standard in expert witness reports, because it is necessary to indicate the basis on which you are giving your opinion.

The opinions in your report could be followed by a listing of the documentation examined in a case. This is not always necessary but can be helpful to a reader of the report. If a case is very small, this is easy. There will likely be a short bulleted list, which outlines certain financial documents used to come to your conclusions.

This might be more difficult in a larger case, and fraud investigators sometimes opt instead to use a printout of their document management database as an attachment to the report. Remember that in most instances of litigation, the opposing attorney will have a right to know on what documents the fraud examiner relied in forming an opinion. A listing of documents examined included with the report can help facilitate this process.

Attachments

Exhibits and attachments are often included with a report on a fraud investigation. Attaching some of the most important or incriminating documents can help a reader understand the report and offers the reader a chance to confirm what has been stated in the body of the report.

Well-organized attachments are a must, and it is especially desirable for the fraud investigator to reference these attachments in the body of the report. The attachments are often numbered (1, 2, 3, etc.) or lettered (A, B, C, etc.) to make referencing them easier. If documents have already been Bates labeled as part of the litigation process, the fraud investigator could instead use those identifying numbers or letters when referencing attachments. Remember that substance rules over form in a fraud investigation. However, even though the actual substance of the attachments is most important, presenting these items neatly will add credibility to the report.

Try to limit the attachments to only the most important pieces of documentation. Hundreds of pages of evidence might be relevant to the report, but not all of them need to be attached or cited as exhibits. Those can be examined separately by an interested party. The attachments to the report should be the most compelling items and the ones that are most critical for the reader of the report to see right away.

Draft Reports

One particularly contentious issue related to the report of a fraud investigator is that of draft reports. Many forensic accountants and fraud investigators prepare drafts of their reports, which are used to present preliminary findings to legal counsel or otherwise begin the process of sorting out the investigative findings. Unfortunately, draft reports create a problem when it comes to the discovery process in litigation. Although the issue is hotly debated, I believe many professionals agree that drafts of the report (especially ones that were shared outside the investigation firm) should be turned over to opposing counsel if requested.

What happens when opposing counsel sees significant differences between the drafts and the final report? Of course, this is a perfect line of questioning for deposition and trial testimony. Instead of just defending the final report, the expert is put in a position of defending the final report and explaining the changes between the draft and the final.

If small changes in wording were made between the draft and the final report, there is not much of an issue. If a final report was created simply because additional information was produced after the draft was created, this is usually not problematic, either. The problem arises when the final report includes or excludes substantial information compared to the draft report. It is not enough to simply say that the investigator changed her or his mind. A rationale must be presented, and there are more issues for opposing counsel to attack.

For example, suppose that some small bit of information might suggest that someone other than the accused was involved in a fraud. The fraud investigator notes this in the draft report, but later determines it is an insignificant point and does not include it in the final report. Opposing counsel might suggest that the fraud investigator excluded this from the final report only in an attempt to cast the defendant in a more negative light. Even if the fraud investigator truly believed the detail was insignificant, her or his objectivity may come into question.

What is the solution to this problem? One solution is to *not* discard any drafts of a report that were shared with parties outside of the fraud investigation firm. If the drafts were completely internal and never shared with an outside party (like the client or the attorney), a good case can probably be made for discarding them as working copies that were used simply to facilitate editing.

To prevent having to retain drafts of reports and ultimately turn them over to opposing counsel, the fraud investigation firm could simply never produce a draft report that is shared outside the firm. As much as the attorney representing your client may want a chance to look at your opinions and ask you to change them, you can refuse to produce a draft.

A preferable option to producing a draft report is a face-to-face meeting with the attorney to discuss what you anticipate including in your final report. This meeting does not include a draft report. Rather, it includes only a verbal discussion of what is likely to be in the report. If no draft is created and shared with counsel, there is nothing to produce during discovery other than that one final version of the report.

Unfavorable Opinions

What happens if a fraud investigator completes her or his work in a case and decides that the opinions she or he has on the case are damaging or detrimental to the party that hired the investigator? For example, suppose a company executive is being accused of defrauding the company of $10 million. The attorney for the executive hires a fraud investigator to analyze all available documentation and determine whether the executive really was responsible for a $10 million theft.

The fraud investigator completes all work and determines that the executive was actually responsible for the theft of $12 million from the

company. What happens? It is not unusual to give legal counsel the
option to terminate the engagement prior to the issuance of an expert
report. The expert is bound by a confidentiality agreement to not reveal
her or his findings to any parties, and walks away from the case.

What if the fraud investigator finds that the executive committed a
$4 million fraud against the company? Before writing a report, she or he
should speak to the attorney to determine how things will be handled.
On the one hand, $4 million is less than the $10 million the executive is being accused of stealing. On the other hand, the attorney may
have been hoping for complete exoneration of the client. The attorney
should be given the opportunity to decide whether an expert report will
be issued.

The fraud investigator should not feel bad if her or his services
are terminated before writing a report. Common sense says that the
investigator is being hired to help one side with a case, and if the
investigator's work doesn't aid that party, there is no reason to write
a report. The worst thing an investigator could do is alter her or his
opinion to make it more favorable to the client. That is unethical and
very risky. Imagine being on the witness stand and having the revised
opinion ripped apart with the real facts in the case.

Follow-up to the Fraud Investigator's Work

After the issuance of the expert report, company management and retained attorneys must decide what to do with the information the fraud
investigator has presented. If the case is already in litigation, the use of
the report is obvious. If the company has not yet taken action, a few
options should be considered.

Internal Discipline

It is natural to want to dismiss an employee as soon as it is apparent
that the person has committed a fraud. It is often safer for the company
to have the suspect off-site, so that no more fraud can occur, but it is

important to realize that this may also hamper the gathering of information. For this reason, some companies decide not to immediately terminate the employee. If the employee is still actively employed by the company when the fraud investigator's report is issued, a decision must be made about her or his future. The company could decide to do nothing if sufficient evidence is not available or if the evidence exonerates the employee.

The next possibility is discipline, while maintaining the person's employment with the company. This might include a warning, suspension, demotion, change of duties, probationary period, or pay cut. Labor and employment attorneys must be involved in this process to ensure that no laws are broken in the process of punishing the employee.

Terminating the employee may be a viable option as well. In companies with strong zero-tolerance policies, this might be the standard reaction to most fraud cases. It is easy to see why management may not want the employee at the company, especially if the company is very small. Trust has been broken, and management may not believe that it can be mended, so the employee is better off terminated.

It is important for management to remember that swiftly disciplining an employee who has engaged in fraud or unethical behavior can have a deterrent effect. Employees may think twice in the future before committing fraud if they know that management takes action in these cases.

Insurance Claims

It is always advisable for a company to check its business insurance policy for coverage related to employee theft. This should be done as soon as a potential fraud is identified. Insurance companies often have clauses that require a fraud to be reported soon after it is suspected, so it is best to contact them immediately. Unfortunately, many companies have no coverage or inadequate coverage for cases of employee dishonesty. An assessment of risk goes with the purchase of every insurance policy, and lower coverage (or no coverage) for internal fraud is a risk that management may be willing to take.

The fraud investigator's report should be sufficient to substantiate an insurance claim by the company. The claims process can often be made easier if the company puts insurance company claims personnel directly into contact with the fraud investigator. In this way, any questions or concerns can be resolved quickly.

Civil Legal Action

Upon gathering evidence to support an opinion on allegations of fraud, a company may decide that pursuing a civil suit against the perpetrator is the best course of action. If this happens, a fraud investigator's assistance may be needed to help gather the right documents. During the process of discovery, each side of a case is trying to find out as much as they can about the situation, requesting documents and demanding that certain questions are answered.

A fraud investigator can be a big help in putting together a request for production of documents. Because the investigator has familiarity with the case, she or he is in a good position to know what documents could bolster the case and fill in any holes discovered during the investigation.

It is important that document requests are specific enough that they clearly identify the information that is being asked for, yet not so specific that the company or person responding can avoid providing the documents. For example, certain ledgers or accounting records may have common names, yet be called by a company-specific identifier. It is important to identify those records by both the common name and the company-specific name (if known), so that the opposition cannot say they don't know what is being requested.

Criminal Charges

A defrauded person or company can refer a case to law enforcement and can help increase the chances of the case being prosecuted but ultimately does not make the decision to prosecute. That decision lies solely in the hands of law enforcement. The larger the fraud or the more egregious the case, the more likely that law enforcement may seriously look at it. Local law enforcement is often reluctant to get involved with white-collar crime cases because of lack of resources, lack of expertise, and a focus on violent crimes.

It is more common for the FBI or a state law enforcement agency to give serious consideration to a white-collar case. However, they often do not have a lot of time or resources to devote to an investigation. If the company comes to them with a report from an independent fraud examiner, complete with supporting documentation, it is sometimes easier to get law enforcement to consider the case. Simply put, law enforcement resources are stretched thin at all levels, and the more work the company can do for law enforcement, the easier it might be to have them consider criminal charges.

Being an Expert Witness

Fraud investigators generally get involved in fraud investigations with the knowledge that they may very well end up in court, testifying as an expert witness. Unlike a traditional auditor, who looks at the numbers, issues a report, and is essentially done until next year, the fraud investigator knows that there may be court activity in her or his future.

For this reason, it is important that all work be completed and documented with the potential for litigation in mind. At some point, the expert witness will be required to produce her or his file for the matter, and it is important that it include only the things that should be in there. I'm not suggesting that anything in a fraud investigator's file be discarded. Rather, I am in favor of carefully adding items to the file. As explained in earlier chapters, there are best practices related to organizing documents, taking notes on meetings, and creating worksheets to help with your financial analysis.

Preparing for Testimony

When a fraud case goes to court, either civilly or criminally, the fraud investigator has to be ready to testify at deposition, trial, or both. If you have a chance to prepare for deposition or trial testimony with the attorney with whom you are working, you should take it. It is never a bad idea to walk through possible lines of questioning and practice your answers, especially if you have never testified before or if you are still relatively new at it.

One of the challenges when you are investigating a fraud as a team is making sure that the person giving the testimony is familiar enough with the documents, the findings, and the report. The person who will testify is most often the lead investigator, but naturally, she or he has had help from others and has not seen all of the documents in the case. The testifying expert must trust that the team has fully investigated the important issues in the case and has not missed anything critical. A level of confidence in the team is developed over time, and good evidence handling and document management procedures will help support the expert's testimony.

Preparing for testimony does not mean that you are letting the attorney tell you want to say. You will testify truthfully regardless of what happens during your preparation. But it is helpful if the attorney shares her or his strategy with you and helps you focus your testimony accordingly. If you are new at testimony, you will want to practice letting the attorney ask a question and not answering until the attorney is finished with the question. It is human nature to begin answering partway through the question, but the court reporter can take down the words of only one person at a time. It sounds easy to wait your turn to speak, but it does take a bit of practice.

It is also a good time to consider things that opposing counsel might bring up to diminish your credibility, as well as problems in your report that might be brought up during testimony. Consider what you would criticize if you worked for the other side. If you are aware of weaknesses in your opinions or your analysis, it makes sense to talk it through and be prepared for the criticism.

If a case ends up making it to trial, it is a good idea to go through your testimony again with the attorney. You will know what opposing counsel is zeroing in on, based on your deposition. You can again walk through the strategy, address the weaknesses in your report and deposition testimony, and generally prepare for the courtroom experience.

Deposition Testimony

A deposition is a chance for opposing counsel to ask questions about your work and your report. There are not a lot of limits to what can be asked in a deposition. Opposing counsel's goal in the deposition is to get the expert to state exactly what her or his opinions are. Any changes between those opinions and what is said during the trial can cause big problems.

All parties should agree on who is paying the expert for the deposition before the day of deposition. In most cases, the party asking for the deposition will have to pay for it. Experts often bill hourly for deposition time, but some experts also use minimum charges or charge in blocks of time (four-hour blocks or eight-hour blocks are common).

It is common knowledge that experts do not always get paid for depositions, especially when the opposition is responsible for the fees. Collecting payment from the opposite side is not always easy. It is not a bad idea to request prepayment, especially in extremely contentious matters. The request has a fair chance of being rejected, but it is still okay to ask. In some jurisdictions, there will be a time limit on your deposition, sometimes two or four hours. In other jurisdictions, there will be no limit on your time, so long as someone is willing to pay for your time.

A deposition is similar to court testimony, but there is no judge present. In a traditional deposition, there will be the expert, a court reporter, opposing counsel, and the attorney on your side of the case. Occasionally, opposing counsel will have an expert present to assist with developing questions for you. Sometimes the plaintiff or defendant will be there to observe, but that is not common. Making video recordings of depositions is becoming more common, so a videographer may be present, too. If the deposition is going on video, the witness must be more careful about appearance, gestures, and demeanor.

The deposition typically starts out with the attorney questioning the fraud investigator about her or his background and credentials. Sometimes the attorney is trying to build a case that you should be disqualified as an expert because you do not know enough or do not have the right experience. If you are confident that you are qualified to render the opinion you're giving, don't be frightened or offended by this line of questioning. Remember that it is the opposing attorney's job to rattle you and get you to doubt yourself so you do not testify well. Do not fall into that trap.

The rest of the deposition will focus on the expert's analysis and report. Some attorneys work methodically through the report, asking questions about each opinion and the work that happened prior to forming that opinion. Others are not so methodical and do not plan their time well. They may spend hours belaboring certain small points in the expert's work, and you may leave the deposition wondering why you were not questioned about the parts of your work that you thought were most important.

It is not necessary to try to outsmart an attorney or try to predict what questions are coming. Answer the current question carefully and truthfully. Yes, attorneys do try to set traps for experts, but even if you accidentally fall into one of them, there is a way out of it. If you have answered truthfully, the attorney on your side of the case can find a chance to clarify your answers.

Take your time in answering questions to be sure that you are offering a precise answer to exactly what was asked. There is nothing wrong with pausing to formulate your answer in your mind before you speak. Unless there is a video camera present, no one will know how long you paused when they are later reading the transcript. Use that fact to your advantage and think carefully before you answer.

Do not be too quick to agree with a hypothetical situation or a paraphrase of your testimony. You are not required to agree to anything in the deposition, and if you believe a paraphrase mischaracterizes the precise answer you gave, then do not agree to the paraphrase. It may be difficult to stand your ground when an attorney is trying to bully you into agreeing that one phrase means the same thing as another phrase. If it does not mean the same thing, do not allow yourself to be coerced into saying that it does. You have a right to have your testimony on the record exactly as you spoke it, not as opposing counsel rewords it.

The witness can answer hypothetical questions, but should be sure to indicate that it is a hypothetical situation and not the situation that you investigated. Often, opposing counsel will change some facts of the case and ask whether that would change the investigator's opinion. Many times the answer is a truthful "yes." Of course the opinion could change if the facts change. Do not be quick to agree to hypotheticals, but do not be horrified if you ultimately end up agreeing with the attorney's conclusion to the hypothetical.

If you are asked to consider other numbers in your analysis and to recalculate things, do not be afraid to ask for a break to do that. It is not always easy to work with your calculator with all eyes on you, so a break might be appropriate to do the calculations. Also, if the new calculations require a spreadsheet or a detailed calculation, you should say that. You cannot be forced to do a sloppy or incomplete calculation at that moment, and you can refuse to do so.

Sometimes the attorney questioning you in the deposition is making a mistake when formulating questions, is referring to the wrong piece of paper, or is missing a key piece of information that would help her or him. You are under no obligation to volunteer information or otherwise help opposing counsel. There are times when it makes sense to clarify a point so the deposition can move forward. Many times, however, the deponent should not volunteer information. The burden is on the attorney to ask the right questions. If she or he does not, that is not the deponent's responsibility.

And what happens if opposing counsel finds a mistake in your work and points it out during the deposition? If there is in fact a mistake, you will have to admit it, but we all make mistakes, and you just need to figure out how to deal with it. Hopefully it is a minor clerical error or an instance of a small number being accidentally excluded from your analysis. Whether the error is big or small, you will have to recalculate things and determine whether your opinion should change. It sounds horrible, and it may be embarrassing, but it would be even worse to carry on some charade that suggests you did not make an error. Admit the error gracefully and explain what the impact is on your numbers and conclusions.

Following your deposition, you should be given a copy of the transcript so you can review it for accuracy. Court reporters do make mistakes in taking down the testimony, and it is important for you to correct them, especially if the mistakes have a real impact on the numbers or opinions. Imagine how a transposed number in a transcript might cause problems at trial. It is important to get something like that corrected right away.

Trial Testimony

The vast majority of cases are settled before trial, so the opportunity to testify at trial does not come along often. The expert must examine the transcript from the deposition so that she or he is sure of the answers that were given to questions. It is important that trial testimony not conflict with what was said during the deposition. If you later find that you made an error in your deposition testimony, you should immediately bring this to the attention of the attorney with whom you are working. The attorney will need to figure out how to deal with this issue and does not want to be surprised by this information when you are on the witness stand at trial.

Your demeanor and attitude on the witness stand will be very important during trial testimony. A good expert has an air of confidence, without arrogance. She or he is professional at all times, not casual or sarcastic. The best experts are not evasive in their answers. They get their points across clearly and succinctly. A good expert answers just the question asked, and pauses before answering questions in case the attorney she or he is working with needs to object to a question. Judges and juries respond well to answers that sound conversational, not scripted. They appreciate honesty and are generally willing to learn if your testimony is broken down into lay terms.

There are differing opinions on whether the expert should look at the jury during testimony. Some expert witnesses never look at the jury, while others suggest that all testimony should be directed toward the jury. I suggest a more middle-of-the-road approach. The expert should look toward the jury when it feels comfortable, and alternately direct answers toward the attorney asking the questions or the judge, as appropriate. It is more important to act relaxed and natural than it is to rigidly look at a particular person in the courtroom.

Do not get flustered if you make a mistake during testimony or you feel that opposing counsel "got you" on any points. The attorney on your side of the case should be alert and should offer you an opportunity to correct or explain any answers you gave. Again, so long as you do your best to tell the truth in your testimony, you will likely do well on the stand.

Following deposition and trial testimony, it is a good idea to debrief with the attorney with whom you worked during the case. There is always something to be learned, and you should ask the attorney where you excelled and what you might have done differently.

Note

1. Relating to the legal process of discovery, in which parties to the case are required to turn over certain documentation and evidence relative to the case. An attorney may wish to delay the writing of a report in order that the findings of the investigation not yet be turned over to the other side.

CHAPTER 12

Other Issues

There are some practical matters related to investigating fraud that do not really fit into a discussion of how to perform a fraud investigation but are important to examine anyway. Consider this chapter a catch-all part of the book, designed to address some of the issues fraud investigators will experience in the performance of their work.

Moving Forward as a Company

After a fraud is discovered and fully investigated, a company and its employees must move forward. That might seem like a simple thing to do, but it is not always quite that easy. The financial blow of an internal fraud can be devastating. Employees have long-term memories that may not allow them to forget about the violation of their trust by someone who worked side-by-side with them or by someone who was responsible for their future.

The most obvious potential long-term effect from an employee theft is financial devastation. Experts on corporate fraud estimate that the average company loses 7% of its revenue to internal fraud each year.[1] Imagine how many companies could be put out of business with a fraud of that size. The first step to moving beyond an internal fraud, especially a significant fraud, is repairing the financial damage. Often, cash reserves have been depleted and debts have mounted while the dishonest employee was filling her or his pockets. A plan to repair the company's finances should be established quickly.

One prime financial consideration is the effect the fraud may have on the company's relationship with its bank. Loan covenants are often violated when a substantial fraud has been committed and it is important that a realistic and well-thought-out financial recovery plan is presented to the bank. The company needs a commitment from the bank regarding future financing, and a plan will be required to proceed with this commitment.

The financial plan should include an analysis of the company's current cash, receivables, and debts. Information on the theft should be compiled and presented in conjunction with the historical financial statements, highlighting what the financial statements would have looked like without the theft. A thorough analysis of projected sales, profits, and cash flow should be done to determine whether the company can survive the loss.

When making projections following a fraud loss, there is a temptation to be aggressive in estimating future sales and profits. While that might be helpful in securing a financing commitment from the bank initially, it will cause problems down the road if the company falls short of those numbers. The better option is to make realistic projections that the company has a good chance of achieving.

The next step in recovering from a fraud loss is determining the impact the loss has had on employees. One of the most devastating effects of an internal theft can be the negative impact on employee morale. Employees feel betrayed by the thief, especially those who worked very closely with her or him. A perpetrator of internal fraud does not just steal from a company. She or he steals from every honest employee who works there. Employees may think about the raises that were too small or the bonuses that were not given and believe that the thief had a lot to do with that. (And they are probably right.)

Employees should be given some information about the theft, so they are not left wondering what happened. It is important not to jeopardize an investigation or court case, but some basic information can be provided without damaging the case. At the same time that the information is provided, management should affirm their commitment to emerging from the crisis and playing as a team. Management should also communicate the efforts to develop better controls and prevent future frauds.

Preventing Future Frauds

Moving forward after an internal fraud requires that management actually make good on those promises to prevent future frauds. It is sometimes difficult to get management to make changes, because they view changes as another cost on top of the cost of the fraud and the investigation. But shoring up internal controls is necessary if the company really wants to improve after a fraud.

The wise members of company management are interested in re-mediation after an internal fraud is discovered, and often they look to the fraud investigator for guidance in this area. It makes sense to have someone well versed in fraud schemes help management make improvements for the future.

Naturally, the vulnerabilities in the company's system revealed after the theft should be addressed first, and any holes in the system should be closed. Job duties should be analyzed, and some tasks may need to be reassigned to prevent any single employee from having too much control over a function. Segregating duties is one of the most basic fraud prevention controls that all companies should implement, and in reality this is a very cheap method of fraud prevention if it is done correctly.

Management should strongly consider establishing a fraud hotline. It is an inexpensive way to offer employees an anonymous, confidential method to report suspected fraud. Statistics show that an employee tip is one of the most common ways internal fraud is discovered, and a hotline helps facilitate the reporting of fraud.

More extensive fraud prevention measures include creating stronger internal controls and completing regular audits of vulnerable areas of the company. If done correctly and thoroughly, this process can be time-consuming, but it is typically a worthwhile investment, because bad internal controls are nearly useless.

Managing the fraud risk when there has been an executive-directed fraud is often more difficult. It involves the employees who have the most control over everyone and everything at the company. If the CEO wants something done, most times it is going to get done whether out of employees' fear or obedience. Upper management fraud often can be stopped only through stronger corporate governance. This deals more with independent oversight of management and operations, rather than managing detailed transactions and interactions.

Improved corporate governance means better oversight of management via a board of directors with independent members who have no employment or other material relationship with the company. If these board members are truly independent, they are more likely to take action when suspicions of fraud or unethical behavior are raised. The board must be committed to ethical behavior from all employees at all times. They must exhibit the type of behavior they expect, thereby setting the tone at the top. The board must be willing to investigate allegations of fraud or inappropriate behavior. They must not be thwarted by management, exercising their own judgment in determining what must be investigated.

In addition to independent directors, good corporate governance requires an audit committee with financially literate members and at least one financial expert. The audit committee must also have the authority to initiate investigations and seek legal counsel and advice as it deems necessary.

The nominating and compensation committees of the board of directors also must be comprised of independent directors who have no vested interest in their decisions. When compensation is tied to the company's financial performance, there may be an incentive of sorts for management to cheat on the financial statements. The compensation committee must balance that risk with the benefit of giving management incentives to grow the company. Boards of directors and committees must meet regularly, and must do so without management being present. This ensures that management does not exert undue influence over the board or the committees.

It is easy to see why management may shy away from the process of fraud prevention, even after being taken advantage of by a dishonest employee. It can become a huge project, and it can cost a lot, depending on how thorough management wants to be with its fraud prevention efforts. But common sense should tell management that they must make an effort to create stronger controls to prevent internal fraud. The next fraud could put the company out of business. It should take only one major fraud for management to have a vested interest in improving fraud prevention within the company.

Marketing a Fraud Investigation Practice

A book on fraud investigations would not be complete without a discussion of how to actually find investigations to do. Those working in-house for a corporation are not going to have that problem. They already have a captive audience. But those who are working as consultants are going to need a client base if they want to investigate anything. Many fraud investigators have the luxury of working for a firm with a wide client base. But plenty of firms are just branching out into fraud investigation and could use some tips on developing a client list.

One of the keys to developing a client base lies in defining the services of the fraud investigation practice. It is easier to market the firm and secure new business when the range of services is narrowed down. Too often, firms generically promote fraud investigation services. As we have already learned, many types of fraud investigations can be done, including financial statement fraud, corporate embezzlement, bribery cases, insurance fraud, and investment scams. Corporate disputes like arguments over contracts or shareholder disagreements can quickly lead to fraud allegations as well.

Some fraud investigators specialize within certain industries, such as healthcare or financial services. Those industries may require specialized knowledge to effectively investigate allegations of fraud, so it makes sense that some fraud investigators concentrate on one or two industries. It is important to be sure that you are clear on where your firm's capabilities lie. What work does your staff and management enjoy doing and at what are they most competent? Where can you build your niche and establish a reputation? What connections do you already have that can assist your business-building efforts in a particular area?

The market for fraud investigation services can be further divided into a variety of clients who might contract with your firm. Clients could include attorneys, corporations, government agencies, nonprofit organizations, or individuals. For example, you may work primarily with attorneys who are litigators at medium-to-large firms. Their work is typically done for corporations that have suspicions of fraud, and they will identify and retain an expert to investigate those allegations.

Other fraud investigators may choose to work closely with government agencies, either in regulatory matters or criminal prosecutions. Still other fraud experts may choose to work with individuals on consumer fraud issues or family law cases. You can see that the choices are almost endless, and it would be difficult to effectively market a firm's services without narrowing down the list of potential clients. It is much easier to craft and deliver a marketing message to only one or two key audiences.

I have found that directing my marketing and advertising efforts toward a narrow audience has been the most effective. I have tried broad marketing initiatives and did not get a whole lot of results from them. When I have narrowed my focus and advertised in industry-specific publications, I have had better results. The results can be attributed to advertisements that spoke more directly to the audience, mentioning specific types of cases or situations with which they might need assistance.

Competing with Other Firms

One of the universal truths in competing with other businesses is that those who focus on what they do best are more likely to succeed. As a small practitioner, I found that I could compete with larger firms by focusing on particular strengths that set my firm apart from run-of-the-mill forensic accounting or fraud investigation firms.

Smaller firms can compete by developing a niche and performing at a very high level within that niche. A smaller fraud investigation firm will have to emphasize and sell the quality behind its services if it wants to compete with mid-sized (and larger) firms. For example, a smaller firm can often provide more direct contact with highly experienced professionals. It is no secret that larger firms often send younger, less experienced staff members to a client site to perform the bulk of the work on an investigation. That business model has worked for the large firms for a long time, but it is not necessarily the best for the client.

Therefore, in my sales pitch, I emphasize to the client that I will be personally involved in all investigative work. Would a client rather have someone more experienced or less experienced working on their case? It is not hard to believe that most clients would prefer a more experienced investigator if given the choice.

The actual marketing of the small firm's niche services will probably rely heavily on the direct involvement of the head of the practice. The lead investigator should probably be featured prominently in advertising and during marketing events. The firm should want potential clients to identify directly with the most experienced investigators—the ones who will be providing that high-quality investigation that will be the key selling point.

Larger firms tend to do a better job with long-term investigations and with investigations that have a global component to them. They have great depth in terms of employees and specialties, and they have a wide geographic presence. Larger firms are much better equipped to deal with massive investigations for very large companies. A very large firm with offices around the world can almost always round up an expert on any issue or in any industry.

Conducting a Global Investigation

As discussed in Chapter 9, the Foreign Corrupt Practices Act (FCPA) is a major concern for American companies. The instance of global investigations has been increasing, and the number is likely to continue to grow in the long-term. Probably the most important part of a global investigation is assigning employees who have familiarity with local issues. The lead investigator should be able to quickly send investigators to global locations and should have the ability to secure local resources to aid in the investigation.

Basic fraud investigation skills do not change from country to country. Many of the most common fraud risks cross all borders, but there will always be local customs or business practices that could add special fraud risks. Language and cultural barriers should not be underestimated, and the fraud investigator should be aware of any special challenges in securing documentation and evidence in a foreign country.

One of the worst things a fraud investigator can do is insult another culture or make faulty assumptions about the way another culture does business. Larger fraud investigation firms are often better equipped to execute international investigations, because they have a diverse staff, which has a greater chance of being familiar with cultural issues.

An international engagement needs one central coordinator for all work, who will assign regional or local coordinators who will report to her or him. Local or regional coordinators will be responsible for mobilizing local staff or requesting that experienced staff be sent to the location. The best international investigators use a mix of staff that includes local people plus employees stationed in the country in which the client is headquartered. Larger auditing or forensic accounting firms have more experience in international engagements and are likely going to be better prepared to carry out the project. Do not underestimate the depth of experience it takes to manage and execute an engagement that involves multiple countries.

Professional Liability Issues

Any professional engagement always runs the risk of developing malpractice and liability issues. The best way to prevent these types of things from coming up is through a combination of three key points: (1) communication with the client, (2) an engagement letter, and (3) professional competence. All three points may seem to be strongly based in a common sense approach to doing business, but that is not always the case.

Communication with the client is important in order to match your services with their expectations. The professional has to have sufficient communication with the client to determine exactly what the client wants out of the engagement. There are times when the client has unreasonable expectations, and the fraud investigator is obligated to address them before beginning the engagement.

Maybe the client wants the fraud investigator to engage in illegal acts or wants a certain level of proof gathered that is not possible. Sometimes clients want a level of detail examined that does not make sense in light of the cost to do so. At times, clients just do not understand enough about fraud investigations to formulate reasonable expectations.

No matter what the expectations, the fraud investigator has to fully understand them and be willing to say no. Clients do appreciate it when the professional redirects the efforts or suggests a more feasible and cost-effective option. The investigator cannot be afraid to say, "Are you asking me to do X?" And that may be followed by, "I could do that for you, but here is an approach that I think is better, and let me explain why. . . ."

Once the client and the professional have a proper understanding of the needs and desires in regard to the fraud investigation, the next step is creating an *engagement letter*. The engagement letter protects both the client and the fraud investigator and should be viewed as a win-win in that regard.

The level of detail in an engagement letter will likely be determined by the amount of information available at the time it is drafted and the comfort level of the fraud investigator. Some engagement letters explain the work to be completed simply in terms of an analysis of certain documents and creation of a report on the findings. Others will be far more detailed, outlining exactly which documents are going to be examined and specific issues on which the investigator will be giving an opinion.

No matter how detailed the actual work is in the letter, the engagement letter must outline the rights and responsibilities of the parties.

This was covered in Chapter 2, but it bears repeating that the fraud investigator should outline what responsibilities each party has and what will happen if either fails. The professional should have the right to terminate the engagement in the case of nonpayment of fees, noncooperation by the client, or certain other situations. Outlining such things in the engagement letter will protect the professional if the case ultimately cannot be completed.

A seemingly common sense approach to performing a professional engagement is having the proper level of experience and *competence* in the matters being investigated. This may seem to be self-evident, but there are still instances in which a professional accepts a case for which she or he is not qualified.

The problem is more often seen with small fraud investigation practices. Sometimes the professionals are so eager to secure work that they are willing to go outside of their area of experience to provide what the client needs. This is a disservice to the client, who should expect that the professional accepting an engagement is properly experienced and qualified to do the work.

One way for smaller firms to gain experiences with new types of cases or unfamiliar industries is by contracting with other small firms to work jointly on projects. This ensures that the client has a properly experienced investigator on the case, while the other professional gets firsthand experience that can be leveraged in future engagements.

Reducing Fraud with Investigations

When consumers think about investigating fraud, they do not usually think of the investigation as part of an overall plan to reduce fraud in a company. An investigation is typically seen as a reactive process that is engaged in only when a major problem is identified. Fraud investigations are representative of something completely negative, and they should be avoided at all costs, because if we do not have fraud investigations, then we do not have fraud.

The reality is not quite so fatalistic. Fraud investigations can and should be a routine part of a proactive fraud prevention program.

Anti-fraud education and proactive fraud prevention procedures are essential to reducing corporate fraud, but fraud investigations are a third and equally important part of the equation. Even in companies with the most comprehensive fraud prevention policies, procedures, and controls, there will still be some level of fraud. Investigations are needed to thoroughly examine allegations and suspicions of fraud. They also play a deterrent role, as employees are less likely to engage in fraud if they know that periodic checks occur throughout the company.

It would be nice if fraud investigations were to become completely unnecessary, but that is not realistic. In companies with increasingly better anti-fraud controls, the need for reactive investigations should decrease. But fraud investigations should never be completely eliminated, because even the companies with the most effective fraud prevention programs will still have some instances of fraud to investigate. The hope is that incidents requiring a full-blown investigation will be decreased and that management can focus their best efforts on turning a profit instead of examining cases of fraud.

Note

1. 2008 Report to the Nation on Occupational Fraud & Abuse, Association of Certified Fraud Examiners, Austin, TX.

Appendix

Carter Company Investigation

Document Request List

- [ ] Profit and loss statements—5 years
- [ ] Balance sheets—3 years
- [ ] Income tax returns—5 years
- [ ] Sales by month—3 years
- [ ] Monthly sales tax returns—3 years
- [ ] Current aged accounts receivable by customer
- [ ] Bank statements, canceled checks, and deposit slips—2 years
- [ ] Check registers—2 years
- [ ] Year-to-date financial statements

The sample presented here is for illustrative purposes only. It is not intended to be used in any actual fraud investigation or forensic accounting matter.

Water Under the Bridge Inc.

Expense Report Examination

Which employees will be examined?

What time period is being examined?

Is there an expense reporting policy?

What does the company's ethics policy say regarding company expenses?

Document Request List

☐ Credit card statements

☐ Expense reports (digital or paper)

☐ Receipts and supporting documentation

☐ Calendars or schedules for employees

☐ Documentation from travel agency

☐ Proof of reimbursement to employee

The sample presented here is for illustrative purposes only. It is not intended to be used in any actual fraud investigation or forensic accounting matter.

Round Wheels, LLC

Company Background Examination

- ☐ Incorporation or partnership/LLC filing
- ☐ Registered agent
- ☐ Officers, directors, members, shareholders
- ☐ SEC filings—3 years (public company only)
- ☐ Fictitious names, Doing Business As (DBA), trade names
- ☐ Parent company, subsidiaries, divisions, affiliates, and related companies
- ☐ Headquarters and other locations
- ☐ Dun & Bradstreet information
- ☐ Equifax business report
- ☐ Court records
- ☐ Lien and judgment search
- ☐ Real estate and mortgage search
- ☐ Personal property search and UCC filings
- ☐ Patent and trademark ownership
- ☐ Competitor search
- ☐ Media search—newspapers, Internet search engines

The sample presented here is for illustrative purposes only. It is not intended to be used in an actual fraud investigation or forensic accounting matter.

David Martins

Personal Income Investigation

☐ Tax Returns and W-2s

☐ Bank statements and check registers

☐ Investment account statements

☐ Retirement plan statements

☐ Employee stock ownership plan documents

☐ 1099s related to any freelancing or consulting income

☐ Credit card statements

☐ Home mortgage documentation

☐ Automobile lease/purchase documentation

☐ Closing statements for any real estate purchases, sales, or transfers

The sample presented here is for illustrative purposes only. It is not intended to be used in an actual fraud investigation or forensic accounting matter.

Angela Adams Case

Document Inventory

Bates	Date Rec'd	Rec'd From	Document	Description
None	05/31/08	Atty Edwards	Complaint	
None	05/31/08	Atty Edwards	Defendant's response	
AA001-002	05/31/08	Atty Edwards	Closing Statement	813 N. Hanford
AA003	05/31/08	Atty Edwards	Check	National Bank payable to Angela Adams
AA004	05/31/08	Atty Edwards	Real estate listing	813 N. Hanford
AA005-012	05/31/08	Atty Edwards	Bank statements	Personal account Jan–June 2007
AA013-018	05/31/08	Atty Edwards	Johnson contract	Johnson's services and terms
AA019	05/31/08	Atty Edwards	Johnson advertisement	From yellow pages
JS1-5	04/19/08	Atty Edwards	Listing documents	813 N. Hanford
JS6-17	04/19/08	Atty Edwards	Closing documents	813 N. Hanford
JS18-29	04/19/08	Atty Edwards	Misc correspondence	Emails between Adams and Johnson
JS30	04/19/08	Atty Edwards	Check	Angela Adams payable to Johnson

The sample presented here is for illustrative purposes only. It is not intended to be used in an actual fraud investigation or forensic accounting matter.

Index